Michael Dudok de Wit

Focus Animation

Series Editor:
Giannalberto Bendazzi

The Focus Animation Series aims to provide unique, accessible content that may not otherwise be published. We allow researchers, academics, and professionals the ability to quickly publish high impact, current literature in the field of animation for a global audience.

This series is a fine complement to the existing, robust animation titles available through CRC Press/Focal Press.

Currently an independent scholar, is a former visiting professor of History of Animation at the Nanyang Technological University in Singapore and a former professor at the Università degli Studi di Milano. We welcome any submissions to help grow the wonderful content we are striving to provide to the animation community: giannalbertobendazzi@gmail.com.

Michael Dudok de Wit
A Life in Animation

Andrijana Ružić

CRC Press
Taylor & Francis Group
Boca Raton London New York

CRC Press is an imprint of the
Taylor & Francis Group, an **informa** business

First edition published 2021
by CRC Press
6000 Broken Sound Parkway NW, Suite 300, Boca Raton, FL 33487-2742

and by CRC Press
2 Park Square, Milton Park, Abingdon, Oxon, OX14 4RN

© 2021 Copyright Andrijana Ružić

CRC Press is an imprint of Taylor & Francis Group, LLC

ISBN: 978-1-138-36730-2 (hbk)
ISBN: 978-1-138-36728-9 (pbk)
ISBN: 978-0-429-42987-3 (ebk)

Typeset in Minion
by codeMantra

I dedicate this book to my daughter Helena Emma and my husband Nikola Balj, without whose love and support this book would not have been possible.

Contents

Foreword

Doing animation is really quite simple. And like anything simple, it is really the most difficult thing in the world to do.

BILL TYTLA (1904–1968)

I first met Michael Dudok de Wit at the Richard Purdum Productions in London in the Spring of 1989.

I was a Walt Disney staff animator, and I had travelled out from Hollywood with my colleagues Glen Keane, Andreas Deja and Hans Bacher to help develop a new screen version of Perrault's *La Belle et la Bête* (*Beauty and the Beast*). Richard Purdum and his wife Jill Thomas had long been mainstays of Richard Williams Soho Square studio. Now they had a studio of their own. It was a lovely little Edwardian jewellery box near the British Museum. We worked from an early draft of the story with no musical numbers as yet.

The Walt Disney Studio, their attention so long focused inward, had become attracted to London due to the intense concentration of creative talent drawn there (pun intended) by the boom in high quality animated commercials for the European market. They discovered this during the making of *Who Framed Roger Rabbit*, as well as Tim Burton's *The Nightmare Before Christmas*. Artists from the UK, Germany, Holland, France, Denmark, Ireland, Italy, Zimbabwe and Hong Kong showed a fresh way of looking at old stories. Purdum's *Beauty and the Beast* unit had a number of star animators, such as Paul Demeyer, Teddy Hall, Rick Baker and Michael Dudok de Wit.

Michael is a tall, soft-spoken man in the manner of many of his country and the kind of dad who looks comfortable with a baby harness hanging around his neck. I'm from New York City and Hollywood, so I am accustomed to creative people who can be loudmouth hustlers. By contrast, Michael Dudok de Wit made his opinions known without shouting or braggadocio. Michael's concepts were so good, delivered with such sincerity, you just wound up taking all of them seriously. We were all impressed with his drawing and storytelling skills. He became an important part of the team working right alongside all the top Disney talent. Ultimately, the Walt Disney Studio decided to go in a different direction from what we were doing, and we all went our separate ways. Despite a bumpy start, *Beauty and the Beast* turned out quite well. That's Hollywood.

I returned to America but remained in touch with Michael. I enjoyed his short films *The Monk and the Fish* and *Father and Daughter* and his feature film *The Red Turtle*. Michael is one of those rare film artists who can have a commercial career, maintain high standards for character animation and yet infuse all he does with a very personal vision. Funny how you can click your TV into the middle of an Alfred Hitchcock film, and within thirty seconds, you know it is a Hitchcock film. It does not even have to be one of the iconic scenes. You just know. That is the mark of a great film artist. Michael Dudok de Wit's films are like that. Thank you, Andrijana Ružić, for writing such a fascinating book. Now let's read on and learn more about the life of this extraordinary animator.

Tom Sito,
Los Angeles, June 2019

Acknowledgements

THE IDEA FOR THIS book germinated in the summer of 2017, in the magical Civita di Bagnoregio situated in central Italy. This antique Etruscan village, constructed on the plateau of an orange-coloured eroded hill, hosts every year a small festival dedicated to the arts of animation and comics, called *La città incantata*. In 2017, Michael Dudok de Wit was the festival's guest of honour. His first feature film *The Red Turtle* (2016) was screened one warm and starry night at the open-air cinema and was enriched the following day by the filmmaker's insightful lecture on the art of film language in *The Red Turtle*. Enchanted both by the feature and the director's lecture, I made a small internet research to find out that several of his short films were analysed in several fine books on animation but that there was not a single one about Dudok de Wit's complete body of work. And one spontaneous question came to my mind: "How was that possible?"

I immediately called up Giannalberto Bendazzi, my professor of History of Animation course at the Milan State University, now a dear friend and a constant source of inspiration. He was the person who introduced me to Dudok de Wit's short films in the first place. In his laconic manner, Bendazzi answered my question with another one: "Why don't you try to write it?" So no sooner said than done, I started with my research by the end of that summer. In the meantime, Giannalberto Bendazzi has encouraged me immensely in this endeavour, and to him goes my very first thank-you on this gratitude list.

I'd like to thank Tom Sito for having written such a nice foreword and спасибо to Yuri Norstein for his meditative review on Dudok de Wit's oeuvre that seemed perfect for this book's epilogue. My gratitude also goes to my friend Olivier Delacroix who gave his inestimable contribution as a proofreader of all my texts. I owe so much to Jelena Balj who helped me with translations from the Dutch and Sanja Đoković from the Russian language. Thank you dear Arielle Basset Dudok de Wit for your kindness, constant encouragement and the loving hospitality you offered me in London.

I'm also very grateful to the following persons who have influenced, enriched and broadened my understanding of animation medium in the last few years. Some of them contributed to the making of this book, while others simply encouraged me, and that meant really a lot. So, thank you, in alphabetical order: Mihail Aldashin, Margit Buba Antauer, Myriam Bardino, Marco Bellano, Serge Besset, Olga Bobrowska, Cinzia Bottini, Marie Bouchet, Bruno Bozzetto, Paola Bristot, Rastko Ćirić, Julien De Man, Guy Delisle, Francesco Dicuonzo, Borivoj Dovniković Bordo, Paul Driessen, Piotr Dumała, Zoran Đukanović, Nikica Gilić, Igor Grubić, Ed Hooks, Claire Jennings, Céline Kélépikis, Igor Kovalyov, Biljana Labović, Heidi Mancino, Simone Massi, Angelina Mrakić, Ilan Nguyên, Laurent Perez del Mar, Cettina Caliò Perroni, Sergio Claudio Perroni, Jill and Richard Purdum, Chris Robinson, Normand Roger, my parents Slavica and Milan Ružić, Aleksandar V. Stefanović, Willem Thijssen, Dragana Todorović, Hrvoje Turković, Ljiljana Vukotić, Arjan Wilschut, Paul Williams and Oscar Zarate.

But most of all my gratitude goes to Michael Dudok de Wit for his endless patience, generosity and confidence. He always found the time to answer all my questions and to clarify all my doubts. He also largely contributed to the genesis of this book, and I actually consider him a co-author.

Andrijana Ružić
Milano, April 2020

Author

Andrijana Ružić graduated in History and Criticism of Art at the Università degli Studi in Milan, Italy, where she fell in love with the medium of animation. She specialised in the History of Animated Film under Giannalberto Bendazzi's mentorship: the subject of her master's thesis was the opus of two unpredictable spirits of the American independent animation scene, John and Faith Hubley, and their Storyboard Studio in NYC. As an independent scholar, she participated in numerous conferences for animation studies presenting the works of diverse independent authors of animation. Since 2012, she has curated the section dedicated to animated films at the International Comics Festival in Belgrade, Serbia. She is a member of the Selection Board of Animafest Scanner, the symposium for Contemporary Animation Studies at the World Festival of Animated Film held annually in Zagreb, Croatia. She writes about animation and art for the Belgrade weekly magazine *Vreme*.

Epigraph

Be the first to see what you see as you see it.

ROBERT BRESSON

I would like to be eyes, to do what eyes do, moving so very far away in an instant, to where the rest of me would never set foot, and everything they see they manage to have whilst leaving it where it is, to possess it without bringing it back, to know it without demanding its attention. I would like to have a boundless touch of the gaze, which knows how to touch everything without being felt, to love without allowing itself to be wounded, to conquer all without having to sacrifice a thing.

I Sometimes Enter Your Gaze.

SERGIO CLAUDIO PERRONI[1]

Michael Dudok de Wit

PHOTOGRAPH TAKEN BY GERARD CASSADÒ

Introduction

SILENCE AND STILLNESS ARE Michael Dudok de Wit's artistic virtues, and they pour out from his personal films evoking the feeling of timelessness. Although all his films transcend the mere chronicling of everyday life, they are rooted in reality, and at the same time, they invoke lyrical reflections about the beauty of time that goes on and on. An excellent draughtsman and a refined observer, Dudok de Wit crafted numerous and snappy advertisements and slow-paced, personal films about the beauty of nature, life and transience. His films contain the wit in the Chaplinesque movements of his characters and the sublime beauty of vast landscapes in which they are immersed. The highlights of his career are distinguished by profound professional and existential crises and overwhelming international acclamations. His unadorned drawings reflect themselves vaguely in Hergé's clear line, whilst his watercolour settings, inspired by compositions from Rembrandt's etchings and Hakuin's artwork, evoke transcendence and spirituality. Dudok de Wit continuously seeks for the formal perfection in his films knowing all the time that he would fail to attain it.

Some time ago, during my internet research for this book, I came across an unusual video portrait of the filmmaker on YouTube. A timeline of "Cinématon", a work-in-progress video project directed by the French artist Gérard Courant, contained one video clip entitled *#1865, Michael Dudok de Wit, Hollande Cineaste, recorded in Aubagne (France), on 30 November 1997* *at 15:30.*[2] In this silent four-minute colour film portrait, Dudok de Wit appears mindful and serene. He has some difficulty to look straight into the camera because of the direct sunlight, but nevertheless he persists. His gaze is calm and a bit melancholic, revealing at the same time a daydreamer and a very self-confident person. We're in 1997, and this forty-four-year-old *Hollande Cineaste* had directed *Tom Sweep* (pilot film) and *The Monk and the Fish*, an auteur short film. Before and between each film, he did a lot of commercials for television, learning about visual efficiency and constantly pushing his limits.

With his most famous film *Father and Daughter*, he won all Grand Prix on every possible festival at which it was shown in competition. Animation historian Giannalberto Bendazzi defined it as "the ultimate auteur film"[3] and not without a reason. Dudok de Wit's semi-abstract film *The Aroma of Tea*, enriched by the music of Arcangelo Corelli, appears to be a sort of a conceptual preparation for his first feature film *The Red Turtle*, completed in 2016 and presented on Cannes Film Festival in the same year. This multi-awarded feature, with Studio Ghibli, Why Not Productions and Wild Bunch as main producers and Prima Linea Productions as a line producer, expresses once again the elaboration of Dudok de Wit's recurrent themes of longing, ultimate desire and ultimate question.

Dudok de Wit is proud of every single frame he has drawn so far whether it was destined for his independent film or for a commercial work. In Dudok de Wit's system of values and approach to work, there is no difference between a "high" and a "low" artwork. All his films have an artisanal imprint and are meticulously elaborated: every single phase of animation is meditated over the storyboards for a long time. His films are immediately recognizable and distinguished by his particular sense for timing, refined colour palette, interaction of light and shadows, absence of dialogues and presence of cyclic time, carefully chosen scores, extended melancholic landscapes and spiritual, meditative contents. Every Dudok de Wit's film is a perfection of a kind: nothing to add, nothing to take away. The key to success for his artistic achievements lies in a perfect balance between limitless and extraordinary intuition and his powerful, vast and elegant rational side.[4]

I have had the opportunity to accompany Michael Dudok de Wit on several animation festivals in which the most interesting moments were the screenings of his films when one could feel the audience's direct reactions. I will never forget a short train ride from a small Italian city of Udine to the queen of all cities, Venice, where the filmmaker was supposed to give a masterclass about his first feature film *The Red Turtle*. The morning train was packed with the buzz of commuters talking on their mobile phones. And then, out of the blue, a middle-aged woman approached us shyly: "Are you the director of the film *The Red Turtle* I have seen last night at the cinema in Udine?" Dudok de Wit nodded, with his typical serene smile. And then the woman burst into tears: "Thank you very much … your film, she whispered, I was so deeply touched by it, and I still am, as you can see". She was visibly uncomfortable for not being able to control her emotions. The audience is touched by Dudok de Wit's films, by their timeless issues and expressive formal grace. His films can be compared to poems full of joyful hope for the mankind, some sort of a chorale paean in praise of life's mystery.

I have realised that Dudok de Wit's art, both commissioned and personal films and book illustrations, have imperceptibly evolved through the passing of time. A certain repertoire of motifs, signifiers, repetitions and visual details that will appear in all his later films originate from his graduation film *The Interview* (1978). Issues like life, death, relationships, laws of nature, perpetual quest for the truth in spirituality are already present in *The Interview*. However, its protagonist will not appear anymore in the filmmaker's future filmography thus leaving space to other characters: monk, father, daughter, travelling dot, survivor on the desert island. Dudok de Wit's draftsmanship lies in a special quality of his line, at times trembling and very fine in graphite, at other times thick and calligraphic in ink. His films are characterised by a series of recurrent visual motifs: the treatment of shadows; typically *dudokesque* diagonal compositions; representations of elements of nature and predilection for the night, moonlight and dark dreams that always have a spiritual ending. Dudok de Wit's personalised film universe, thematically and visually coherent, is not about messages; it is all about questions. And questions grow out of the solitude of his characters.

In 2018, when I visited him for the first time in his London studio, clearly prejudiced with the stories about artists who never stop creating, I was surprised to discover that he doesn't feel the need to draw every day, at least when he's not working full time on a film or doing commissioned illustrations. After the release of his first feature *The Red Turtle* in 2016, he has been travelling incessantly to help the film's promotion or has been giving masterclasses all around the world. But when he's in his London home, between two journeys, he simply enjoys the tranquility and simplicity of everyday life. And yet again, I shouldn't have been surprised by these temporary drawing absences since Dudok de Wit has always had a good equilibrium of his agenda. With the inherited protestant working ethics, he alternates a tranquil and simple living in his London home with frenzy film production rhythms generated by the stressful deadlines. Dudok de Wit is all about this union of a savvy attitude towards his profession intertwined with his pure, genuine and childlike artistic being.

He always listens very carefully to his interlocutor, and when he responds in English,[5] which is his adoptive language, he insists on transparency and incisiveness of words, trying to distillate them as if they were drawings. The provisional title of this book was *Michael Dudok de Wit. The One Who Aims at Perfection,* and when I mentioned this in our conversation, he just stood there for a moment, in silence. And I started to feel a bit uncomfortable. Then, with a gaze of a perplexed child, he finally pronounced: Don't you find that the title sounds a way too arrogant in relation to my fellow animators? I know a lot of them who are constantly pushing their limits to obtain the best possible results in their films. I'm not the only director who wants his film to be perfect.

The book that you're holding in your hands is a unique survey on the career and private life of the animation director Michael Dudok de Wit. It is mainly based on my Zagreb and London interviews with the director from 2017 and 2018 respectively and on hundreds of emails I have exchanged with him in the last four years. It will introduce for the first time a complete overview of the well-defined (but far from being definitive) and canonic opus of this humble genius to the public he belongs to. Visually and thematically, his poetic and unique style of animation has always differed from the rest of the contemporary independent animation production. This monograph will reveal what still challenges and thrills Dudok de Wit in the art of animation and why he continues to believe in the beauty of the hand-drawn animation.

Conceived in a canonical order, this book contains his early biography along with career highlights embedded within six chapters that follow the course of his filmography. In all this, I have tried to shed light on his method of work along with his aesthetical and inspirational sources. I haven't insisted on metaphorical interpretation of his films, having in mind Norman McLaren's observation that every spectator incorporates his/her life experience into a film. I have also included glimpses of his private life, although he himself was not very convinced that this would add anything of particular importance for the fruition and evaluation of his films. Additional materials, such as the *Glossary*, *My Favourite Films* or *Proust's Questionnaire* reveal Dudok de Wit's observations about various aspects of filmmaking as well as his personal taste in arts in general. Recollections and colourful voices of his numerous collaborators, other filmmakers, film critics and animation scholars contribute to better define both the work and the man standing behind such timeless films as *Father and Daughter* and *The Red Turtle*. And finally, my wishful thinking is that this book finds its way to animation neophytes who still haven't discovered this peculiar and much underestimated art form and that they always "experience animated images first as an emotion".[6]

Andrijana Ružić
Milano, April 2020

NOTES

1. Perroni, Sergio Claudio, Entro a volte nel tuo sonno, *La Nave del Teseo, Milano, 2018, p. 28. Translated from Italian by Andrijana Ružić.*

2. Courant, Gérard, *Michael Dudok de Wit* (1997), Cinématon #1865, https://www.youtube.com/watch?v=rivTJnRQgmg, retrieved December 7, 2017.

3. Bendazzi, Giannalberto, *Animation: A World History, Volume* III, Abingdon, Routledge, 2015, p. 114.

4. Spectrum, Contender Conversations, *Michael Dudok de Wit: Intuition vs Reason*, February 6, 2017. https://www.youtube.com/watch?v=Ir45I0pCu6M, retrieved December 7, 2017.

5. His bilingual linguistic origins are in Dutch and French.

6. Kitson, Clare, *Yuri Norstein and Tale of Tales. An Animator"s Journey*, Indiana University Press, Bloomington, 2005, p. 86.

CHAPTER 1

Biographical Notes

There are some things which cannot be learned quickly, and time, which is all we have, must be paid heavily for their acquiring. They are the very simplest things and because it takes a man's life to know them, the little new that each man gets from life is very costly and the only heritage he has to leave.[1]

ERNEST HEMINGWAY IN *DEATH IN THE AFTERNOON*[1]

1.1 EARLY LIFE IN THE NETHERLANDS – A PRIVATE ARCADIA

Michael Dudok de Wit was born on 15 July 1953 in Abcoude, a small village south of Amsterdam, as a second child in a family of long-standing protestant tradition. His father, Robert Dudok de Wit, the descendent of a 17th century old Huguenot family of French origins, was trading in raw sugar, perpetuating a traditional family business passed on over nine generations. His mother, Mireille, originally from Lausanne, Switzerland, gave birth to four sons. In 1954, his parents decided to move to the scenic village of Laren, near Hilversum, a city located in the province of North Holland. The family lived in the serene atmosphere of an old brick house immersed in a vast garden and a small coniferous grove, surrounded by heathland, meadows and canals.

> My father commuted every day to his office in Amsterdam, as regular as a clock, and my mother chose to be a full-time mother and a housewife. Family life was structured by regularity, security and comfortable habits. My parents were a beautiful couple. They didn't believe in disagreements and they constantly strived for kindness and harmony. I admired them and I aspired to become like them. One of my mother's gifts was to create an ambience of friendly elegance at home. She was romantic and I was too, but of course, I had to learn eventually to adjust to real life.[2]

One of his first memory consists of a dream that stuck with him forever. He was sleeping temporarily in his parents' bedroom, so he must have been really small.

> I woke up from a dream, a sort of abstract nightmare. In this dream I witnessed huge dark cubes drifting across the sky and the sight was both terrifying and fascinating. Thinking back, I still consider it a strange dream.

The four boys grew up in a post-war period that was full of optimism since the last traces of the Second World War had completely vanished. The school that young Dudok de Wit attended was also his father's school, situated only one kilometer away from the family house. The neighbourhood was safe, and everybody knew each other. As soon as a child learned to cycle, he/she could ride a bicycle wherever they wanted. "The society where everybody cycles has an easy, natural homogeneity. Everybody has a bicycle in the Netherlands. In that sense, it's a socialist country at heart", said the filmmaker. He and his brothers grew up as bilingual children, with a Dutch and Swiss cultural background. Even if she was very fluent in Dutch, his mother Mireille spoke French with her children. This was unusual at the time and made him feel different, an "outsider".

> In the early school years I was the only bilingual child in my class and the only one who travelled abroad in the summer. Travelling was still a relatively new phenomenon back then. Even during my early adolescence I felt that I had one foot in the Netherlands and one outside, which I really liked.

The family travelled to French and Italian beaches for the summer and went skiing in the winter. They often went to Switzerland, where his mother grew up, in an old house near Lake Geneva. The young man loved staying at his grandmother's home where he would live in "an atmosphere of togetherness with cousins, uncles and aunts". With his parents and brothers, he also spent summer days on the long Dutch sandy coast along the North Sea, near the town of Noordwijk. Even if it was always a joyful experience, his parents didn't feel the need to explore the Netherlands more extensively. "We lived in a beautiful village, immersed in nature. We had our garden, and, in a way, we were happy where we were".

Looking after the animals and manual work around the garden, terrariums and water ponds was an essential part of artist's Dutch childhood. The family also had lots of animals: ponies, chickens, ducks, rabbits and guinea pigs. Dudok de Wit would feed them and was rewarded with extra pocket money by his parents. He especially enjoyed paying night visits to the stables where his favorite ponies were kept, on the edge of the small grove. He would talk to them, caress them and breathe in their warm scent. The continuous presence of various domestic animals had a huge creative impact on the boy.

> I had a very physical awareness of nature around me and I believe that this has fed my sensitivity as an animator. For instance, in the behaviour of chickens you recognize

the behaviour of a human being. Chickens have a sense of hierarchy and they have to prove and justify it every day, like we humans do. I would interfere with their hierarchical habits and watch how they would react. I would observe the movements of the cockerel: he was pretending that he was not looking at me, but he was. Another example is motionlessness. All creatures, from the smallest insects to the largest mammals, demonstrated distinctive moments of stillness. They had their unique way of alternating between moving and not moving. Years later I recognized these observations of behavioral timing in my animation.

As an "outsider" child, he often felt the need to not only be alone, but also to reconnect with social life at any given moment. The small community of Laren, the house and the family and the beauty of the Dutch landscape were his private Arcadia.

As a child I was outside a lot. I would cycle to the polder with a bucket, just to catch frogs and aquatic insects from the canals. Later I would sleep in the garden in my cotton tent. I liked the night. I was also fascinated by the ambience of our old house at nights. I would also go in the garden in the evening just for the pleasure of it. We lived near heather moors[3] and I would cycle across the moors to school. They were part of a vast nature reserve, gorgeous in all weather conditions: snow, rain or mist. They would be covered once a year with lavender coloured flowers. The attraction of the flat polder landscape too lies in its vastness, in its infinity. When you cycle there, you are very aware of the sky and the horizon. Faraway in the distance, you spot a tiny profile of a poplar tree or a church bell tower. All this space was exhilarating.

His father was "contained, stable, calm and thoughtful" and was good with architectural drawings and construction work. His mother was "artistic, intuitive, Mediterranean, emotional". She had studied at an art college for a year. Although she was a talented painter-illustrator, her specialties were clay sculpture and ceramic glaze paintings. From early on, children were stimulated to draw, read books and play musical instruments. The young artist very much enjoyed fairy tales, and one of his peak childhood experiences was the discovery of the public library in Laren.

> The library with its wooden bookshelves had this ancient, quiet atmosphere and to come back home with two books to read was such a joy! I was about ten when we got our first TV. Until then, my father would read stories to my brothers and me every Saturday evening. We would sit around the table, making drawing inspired by the stories. Halfway through the evening we were allowed a bottle of Coca Cola, which was kind of exotic.

Among the first stories he read were the comic strips from the weekly magazine *Donald Duck*. His favourite ones were by Carl Barks[4]: "the best stories by far, visually and narratively". The Tintin books by Hergé[5] also met with immediate approval in their home. The family library contained some old books from his parents: Heinrich Hoffmann's[6] cautionary stories for children *Der Struwwelpeter*, Wilhelm Busch's[7] black humoured children picture stories in rhyming couplets *Max & Moritz* and Marten Toonder's[8] books. Dudok de Wit particularly enjoyed reading Dutch books about colonial life in Indonesia and the jungle's evocative magic. For him, Indonesia was the "other Holland", a faraway mysterious country. His adolescence period was marked by school days, drawing activities, solitary bicycle rides, quiet library afternoons and evening readings to his younger brother. The family had a record player in the house, and he remembers enjoying especially Prokofjev's *Peter and the Wolf* and the music of his mother playing the piano. In the Sixties, there was an explosion in popular music and the discovery of bands like The Beatles, but his preferences soon went to rock and blues music:

"My brothers and I loved music. For me, music became a huge doorway to explore my emotions and to understand originality. I'm referring to rock music from the late sixties, early seventies and especially to the explorative music from the British progressive rock groups such as Pink Floyd and Gentle Giant. I also discovered unusual music from other European countries, especially from Germany and the hypnotic intelligence of jazz-rock".

In his teens, he studied languages and sciences at the local gymnasium, but, somehow, his inquisitive and daydreaming nature prevailed. He told his parents: "I want to leave school and discover things in my own way". His mother in particular was very sensitive to her son's aspirations: "Why don't you study arts abroad and have it both ways?" she replied. When his parents offered financial support for his studies, he assembled a portfolio in order to apply to the Beaux Arts in Geneva. Finally, in the autumn of 1974, a young and enthusiastic Dudok de Wit left Holland and moved to Switzerland.

1.2   GENEVA AND "THE INCREDIBLE FREEDOM OF STUDENT LIFE"

Judging from the quality of his portfolio drawings, the École Supérieure des Beaux Arts commission directed the young man to the so called "black and white department" where he attended courses on engraving, etching, woodcut and life drawing. He was fascinated by the manual process involved in printmaking and the preparatory work and rituals that lead to the production of printed art:

> I liked the fact that we had to prepare our materials and that we had to get our hands dirty, and I loved the smells. The final result would always come as a surprise. With printmaking we create our picture in mirror image and this opened my eyes. The mirror image taught me about composition and space.

Aquatint and black and white photography became his new passions. In his engravings, he played with modulations and grain textures and, with photography, he discovered the beauty of film texture. The themes of his early etchings as a student often had an oneiric and surreal nature. Ever since his childhood, he was influenced and inspired by the sublime etchings of the Dutch painter and printmaker Rembrandt van Rijn (1606–1669). In the early Seventies in Europe, the comic strip art form expanded in an incredible way, with new styles and new subjects touching on politics, sex, violence, mysticism, drug-fueled surrealism, madness. During this period, he discovered the art of the Italian comic book artist and illustrator Guido Buzzelli (1927–1992). Vividly impressed by Buzzelli's style especially in depicting madness, Dudok de Wit realised that he wanted to specialise in visual narration. In his spare time, he conceived and drew comic strips for student magazines, experimented with magic markers and discovered the joy of storytelling in pictures. He invented an unnamed character, a very simply designed round-headed humanoid creature, and put him in all sorts of bizarre and comical situations.[9] He came to an awareness for the first time that animated films "combine the beauty and the power of comics and the beauty and power of music".

In 1975, he attended the International festival of animated film in Annecy, France, for the first time and watched all the films, from early morning to midnight. It was a small festival compared to today's format, and the audience would sit in one theatre. Nonetheless, amidst "all the amazing Annecy programs", he discovered artistic freedom, possibilities, but also the traps of film language such as stereotypes, weak stories and feeble endings. The biggest and the most beautiful discovery for the young filmmaker, however, was the lyrical poetry of the film *The Heron and the Crane*, by the Russian animator Yuri Norstein.

> That, for me now, is the most influential animated film of my life. The film is highly poetic with its nostalgic mood and the warm, evocative Russian voice. The character animation is exquisite. The story is told in two dimensions: from left to right and back. That's common in animation,

but, in this film, the two-dimensionality is really effective. I love the different moods of the weather. Yuri Norstein and his spouse and the film's art director Francesca Yarbusova masterfully conveyed the essence of this thin and sad story in a very simple way. You want the heron and the crane to be totally in love – that's the romantic side of me talking – but the film is not telling that.

The Annecy festival gave him the opportunity to meet directors and animators who also made a strong impression on him. It seemed that they were "totally dedicated and proud of their work, without inflated egos and amongst them I really felt at home".

This group of open-minded, ordinary people who were making extraordinary things changed the course of his life. Enchanted by the narrative and visual potential of the animated medium, and the richness and finesse of its multifaceted language, he decided to leave the art college in Geneva and to find an animation course elsewhere. His parents supported him immediately:

> I knew that if I wanted to be an artist, I would give my art a priority and this can be obsessive and pretty relentless. My mother understood my drive towards a creative career, even though the art of short, independent animated films was new and unfamiliar to her.

In Geneva, he also met his lifelong companion, and, at the time, a psychology student, Arielle Basset. Finally, after one year of studies in Geneva, he applied to four animation colleges: in Poland, Belgium, Canada and England.

1.3   ANIMATION STUDIES IN FARNHAM, ENGLAND (1975–1978)

The West Surrey College of Arts and Design in Farnham accepted his application, and in the summer of 1975, Dudok de Wit moved to England. This college was one of the first ones in the UK to offer a full-time animation BA course. As soon as he started learning animation, he became attracted to the film language. He recalled his college years as very chaotic in terms of organisation, which hopefully resulted in a highly individualistic style of the first cohort of six students that graduated there. In the animation department, there was no rigid schedule. Students substantially learned from one another and were strongly encouraged to experiment. Dudok de Wit was very much attracted to the photography department, and although he didn't follow a proper course, he learned about photographic printmaking from the photography students. He bought himself a good SLR camera and started to carry it around:

> I was looking for subjects every day and everywhere, using a standard 50mm lens only, which was sufficient; there was no need for a zoom lens. I had no specific project, but my aim was to understand classic journalistic photography and my main inspirations were Cartier-Bresson and the photography published in *The National Geographic* magazine.

But there was another great passion in those student years in Farnham, and that was music. It continued to be "a whole universe", and he started to hesitate between becoming a musician or an animator. He listened to music all the time, collected records, played the piano keyboard in a student band and got himself an electric guitar.

> Urban blues guitarists were my heroes: BB King, Freddy King, and British guitarists like Eric Clapton and Peter Green. I longed to be in a solid blues band and play solo guitar or keyboards or both, so I said to myself: "OK be serious, either you become an animator or you join a band and become a musician. You cannot do both full time." I was self-taught on the guitar and there was no sign that I would be really good, so I sold it. It was a simple symbolic gesture, confirming my choice.

The animation curriculum included a course on the history of film, and part of the lecture was dedicated to live action films. As soon as he started learning to animate, he became attracted to a film language, which was fairly new to him. "I grew up in a village without a cinema. TV was still very basic, so I was not at all a film connoisseur. I had seen some mainstream films, a few Bergmans and a few Fellinis, but that was all". On this course, Dudok de Wit discovered the creative and emotional aspects of editing, in Michelangelo Antonioni's and Sergej Eisenstein's films in particular, and started to avidly explore the potentialities of live action films, experimental films and Disney films.

1.4   GRADUATION FILM *THE INTERVIEW* (1978)

Animation director Bob Godfrey was Dudok de Wit's mentor, and his unorthodox method of teaching animation was: "stick to the impossible and once you have learnt the rules break them".[10] Godfrey saw the eight-minute graduation film *The Interview* only upon its completion giving advice on request only, thus leaving his student a lot of freedom and autonomy.

> I made the film on my own. While you're making a film, you're vulnerable. You don't want anybody to criticize your fragile choices. I didn't create a storyboard, because I didn't want to hear comments and feedback, fearing that I would lose my passion. It's the only time I got away with making a film without a storyboard. Now I find the storyboard phase essential and also hugely enjoyable.

The Interview is based on Dudok de Wit's round headed character from his student's comic strips, and it contains all the future characteristics of his output. The film tells the story of a little fellow who goes around with his tape recorder asking people questions that could be interpreted as existential questions. Although some of them collaborate, they cannot give him the right answers because he must figure them out for himself. *The Interview* concludes in a beautiful blue dusk scene: standing on the bridge like a tiny white dot in the big night, the protagonist throws away the tape recorder.

The film is constructed in a space filled with round and arched forms, strong diagonals intersected by the shadows of trees and bridge and with the use of a parsimonious gamut of colours. Several scenes stand as initial prototypes for his future films such as the black and white scene with the window and the protagonist's long shadow on the floor, or the bridge in perspective which call to mind some scenes from his short film *The Monk and the Fish*, whereas the scene with the row of thin poplar trees evokes the atmosphere of *Father and Daughter*. The music is taken from an album by an experimental rock group Faust, and the sounds derive from an electric guitar and the registered sounds of the birds and a sound library.

> The story of *The Interview* was created intuitively; I can see it clearly now. This film represents me as I was in my student days, when I started to read spiritual texts from India and East Asia, meditating and discovering about the more subtle qualities in life such as wisdom and serenity. To explore the subtle qualities, in other words to explore the unknown, I could ask for advice from people, but ultimately, I had to find out for myself. This is what the film is telling me now, which was not as obvious to me in those days.

The film was screened in several animation festivals in the student's competition category. Farnham college didn't provide the distribution option for its alumni's films and didn't teach them how to apply for a job or get work experience. "Art college seemed like a safe community where we can explore art, whereas real life outside seemed competitive and insensitive", recalls the artist.

After graduation, he was not interested in prolonging his academic studies. In 1978, he sent his graduation film to the Ottawa animation festival where the Dutch animator and director, Paul Driessen, sat on the pre-selection jury. Driessen remembers:

Michael had sent in his first film which we liked very much because of its simplicity and charm and had voted for at the preselection presentation. Unfortunately it was taken out of the competition because of an organizer's mistake. When I met Michael at the festival itself, I told him about this oversight. He must have been quite disappointed, of course, but he was very generous in forgiving the festival and hoped he would have more success next time. All very typical of Michael: generous, matter-of-fact and not giving up on pursuing his art.[11]

Dudok de Wit actually was very disappointed; showing his graduation film at the Ottawa festival was of great importance to him. He was keen to test his newly acquired animation knowledge and, to do so, actually needed to start from zero. Dudok de Wit returned to the Netherlands. He knew nothing about animation studios or professional life. Fortunately, his older brother suggested that he look up the list of animation studios in the book of European companies at the local chamber of commerce. And it worked.

1.5 EARLY CAREER – BARCELONA AND A MEDITERRANEAN CULTURE WHERE YOU CANNOT BE ALONE, STILL…

In 1978, Dudok de Wit's curious nature and a desire to explore foreign cultures brought him to Barcelona, Spain. He didn't speak a word of the local languages. Still, he was very much attracted to the idea of living and working for a short period of time in the exuberant and sunlit aura of this Mediterranean port. Barcelona could not offer much in those years unfortunately. Michael freelanced for Pegbar Studios and L'Equip studio, doing basic commercial animation, with little feeling of progress. For two months, he freelanced for an American-Catalan studio on an American animated TV series project based on the book *The Lion, the Witch and the Wardrobe*, directed by Robert "Bob"

Balser.[12] But the professional dissatisfaction and additional sense of loneliness caused him to experience the beginning of an existential crisis. He started to doubt about his professional choice.

> For the first time in my life I felt utterly alone inside. It coincided with the start of a deep, mysterious fear that would soon influence my career, because without this fear I would never have been able to make my films. It was clearly part of a growing up process; I had to catch up. After a harmonious and protected childhood I had to face the real, challenging aspects of adult life. Professionally I had to find my own path, my income, a career basically. I didn't have an inspiring role model and I chose to find things out for myself, but meanwhile the pain was numbing. On a deeper level, I started to have intense questions about life, I mean about the real purpose of life and how to reach it, but there were no answers, or rather, I wasn't ready to see them. I was devastated.

In that same year, Dudok de Wit and Arielle Basset, his girlfriend from Geneva, decided to live together. But soon he travelled to Milan, Italy, where he approached Italian animation director Bruno Bozzetto. At the end of the Seventies, the latter was at the peak of his glory with his feature *Allegro non Troppo* (1976), based on his preferred pieces of classical music. But, again, Dudok de Wit's plans are met with disappointment as, at the time, Bozzetto wasn't in need of new collaborators. Despondent, he returned to Barcelona where a letter from a newly established animation studio in England was waiting for him.

NOTES

1. Hemingway, Ernest, *Death in the Afternoon*, Scribner Classics, New York, 1999, p. 153.
2. Michael Dudok de Wit to Andrijana Ružić, London, 6 December 2018. If not marked otherwise, all further Dudok de Wit's quotes derive from this interview.

3. A tract of open uncultivated upland typically covered with heather.
4. Carl Barks (1901–2000) was an American comic book artist specialized in Donald Duck's adventures.
5. Hergé is a pen name of the Belgian cartoonist Georges Rémi (1907–1983). In his fifty years long career, Hergé had created twenty-three albums of adventures of Tintin, a teenage journalist, which were translated in thirty languages and sold in seventy million copies.
6. Heinrich Hoffmann (1809–1894) was a German psychiatrist who published poems, satires and children's books. His most famous children's book was an illustrated collection of rhymed stories, with both amusing and didactic content, entitled *Struwwelpeter* (or Shaggy Peter), published in Germany in 1845.
7. Wilhelm Busch (1832–1908) was a German painter and poet, known for his drawings accompanied by wise and satiric verses.
8. Marten Toonder (1912–2005) was probably one of the most successful Dutch comic strip artists. His most famous character was a kitten Tom Poes whose comic strip adventures gained him a wide popularity in Holland starting from the forties.
9. Three years later, this character, a sort of young Dudok de Wit's alter ego, will become the protagonist of his graduation film *The Interview* (1978).
10. Smurthwaite, Nick, "One Man and His Wobbly Dog", *The Guardian*, 20 April 2001, https://www.theguardian.com/film/2001/apr/20/culture.features2, retrieved 13 December 2018.
11. Paul Driessen's email to Andrijana Ružić, 14 July 2018.
12. Robert Bob Balser (1927–2016) was an American animator and animation director who lived and worked all around Europe. He is mostly remembered as the animation director on George Dunning's feature film *Yellow Submarine* (1968) inspired by the music of The Beatles. In Spain, he directed a visually innovative short *El Sombrero* (1964) akin to the films of the same period done by John and Faith Hubley in New York.

CHAPTER 2

Animating Commercials for Advertising Agencies

2.1 TOWARDS A REALISTIC PERFECTIONISM – RICHARD PURDUM PRODUCTIONS STUDIO IN LONDON

Richard Purdum Productions, an animation studio founded in London in 1979, was in urgent need of young animators. American animator Richard Purdum and his wife and producer Jill Thomas had thought highly of Dudok de Wit's graduation film *The Interview* seen at the London Film festival and decided to offer him a job. After a year of disillusions in Spain, marked by the start of a profound existential crisis and serious professional doubts, a young filmmaker accepted their offer and moved to London to join the Purdums on their new professional adventure.

New animation studios proliferated all over London during the effervescent years of British commercial animation in the late Seventies. Dudok de Wit remembers that "there was a lot of money and creativity in advertising in those years.

Schedules were long and the competition was not unpleasant".[1] Despite frantic business schedules and numerous deadlines, Jill Thomas and Richard Purdum managed to create an inspiring and family-like working atmosphere in their West End studio. Dudok de Wit started his London freelance career as an assistant animator to Richard Purdum and, gradually, throughout the years, became an animation director. He arrived at their studio just after they had started in 1980 and worked with them on and off for about twelve years, making interesting commercials with small teams of artists.

However, during his apprenticeship year at Richard Purdum Productions, he kept on dreaming about his own new film. In his free time, he continued to work on a storyboard about a character who lives in a snowy landscape and fantasises about flying. In the autumn of 1980, he travelled to the National Film Board of Canada in Montreal where he met two distinguished Dutch authors, Paul Driessen and Co Hoedeman, both established animators and directors at the NFB. Dudok de Wit showed his storyboard to the producer and director of the NFB's English animation department, Derek Lamb, and then to Radio Canada, the production company behind Frédérick Back's films. Unfortunately, neither of them accepted the project. Despite this initial failure, he decided to stay near the NFB, hoping that, one day, he might be offered a chance to collaborate. In the meantime, he found work in Montreal as an animator on Gerald Potterton's science fiction film *Heavy Metal* (1981) but had to return to England in order to obtain a work permit for Canada. Another part of Potterton's film was to be completed in Bill Melendez's London studio, and Dudok de Wit decided to join the team. He described the time spent on this juvenile and sexist assemblage project:

> *Heavy Metal* was an ambitious idea: several comic strip styles from the eponymous magazine were transformed into animation, but the general quality level of the

animation was mediocre. My animation there was terrible. I was a real beginner. I did my best to be professional but, for me, my animation had no soul. I wasn't inspired neither by the story nor by the design.[1]

At the beginning of 1981, Dudok de Wit returned to Richard Purdum Productions and continued to absorb the art of Purdum's masterful animation by merely observing and listening. ("Animation is complex and we keep on learning all the time".[1]) He also considered Richard Purdum a stellar animator: "someone who creates extraordinary drawings and who can handle any design. Dick would work on a realistic bear drinking a cup of hot soup, for instance, and the way he animated the complex animal movements was very impressive".[1] In the meantime, he also freelanced for other London-based studios such as Richard Williams Animation, Klacto and Passion pictures. However, his animation style followed a steep learning curve at Richard Purdum Productions. He co-directed all the commercials with Purdum who taught him the necessity to learn from one's own experience. He also learnt another very important lesson there. "How to understand the audience's point of view and meanwhile, how to be very clear about the message of your film, making sure that the largest possible section of the audience will connect with it".[5] He worked closely with very professional editors, sound recorders, musicians and, as a result, became an excellent team player. His dedication to work and gentle and charming nature was appreciated by hard-to-please clients. This is how Jill Purdum commented Dudok de Wit's approach to a teamwork:

In the early days he would turn his hand to anything, whether it was a style he was comfortable with or something that did not come naturally to him. Very soon, clients became familiar with his style and wanted to know he would be working with them and bringing his signature style to their projects. As he developed his skills, he also became a very good teacher and younger artists were always eager to work with him.[2]

Dudok de Wit drew, animated and directed a great number of successful, stylistically diverse and prize-winning commercials for Richard Purdum Productions. "These ads are coherent and they have integrity. I'm proud to have worked on them",[1] pointed out the filmmaker. Actifed cough syrup ads (1985, 1987), with Bob Hoskins providing his voice to little monster-looking germs in the grip of a spectacular coughing fit, won several prizes. An ad for Heinz Salad Cream with an egg that cracks and a lettuce losing its heart, "VW Sunrise" for Volkswagen, and "Noah" for The Irish Lottery were all drawn by hand in traditional 2D animation. A commercial for Macallan Malt Whisky "The Long Sleep" (1990), starring a sleepy barrel and an eager bottle, reveals Dudok de Wit's predilection for diagonal compositions, shadows and watercolour textures, with thick and thin ink brush strokes defining the outlines. Later on, Dudok de Wit directed and animated three commercials for a roof insulation product by the Owens Corning company, who had bought the rights to use the Pink Panther as a main character.

> The Pink Panther did not excite me at all until the day I realised that it was not about him: he had no character, he just walked around. It was all about the interesting graphic shape of his body – a thin, angular body with an expressive tail. That's when I started enjoying it. In a commercial, the product or story could be boring, but there was always something else that was interesting: artistic backgrounds, the quality of light, elegant roundish movements in the animation, something that I could try out and see how far I could go.[1]

In 1988, Richard Purdum Productions promoted the opening of the Tate Gallery, in Liverpool, with their "state-of-the-art ad, in which a number of modern art forms, from Mondrian to

Magritte, metamorphose".[3] Dudok de Wit's contribution consisted of a short sequence in the style of Juan Miro.

The success of an animated commercial is in the balance between graphic appeal, entertaining content and very limited duration (30 seconds). Paul Wells noted that, in the animated advertising business, "large budgets and the need for immediate visual distinctiveness paradoxically enable a high degree of experimentation and the development of new techniques".[3] Keeping the message subtle and mentioning the product only at the end of the commercial was another characteristic of British commercials in the Eighties. Back in those years, animation was used for many adults' products, and there was more creative freedom for animators in terms of sophisticated design and treatment. Dudok de Wit recalled that "everything was hand-drawn and we tried different tools: black ink, colored pencils, dry pastel, wax crayons. And the rostrum camera operators were very keen to invent new tricks".[1] Particularly arduous were the commercials in which advertising agencies would ask animators to emulate the style of unique characters, from children's or adults' books' illustrations alike, and make them move.

Dark, gothic subjects in Edward Gorey's illustrations were particularly challenging to animate, as was the art of Polish painter Andrzej Dudzinski, whose visual aesthetics was emulated in the Smarties commercial called "Smart-illusions" (1995). Jill Thomas explained that Dudzinski's very rendered style was extremely difficult to translate into a technique that could be animated. Hence Dudok de Wit worked closely with the artist and directed a team of animators and renderers with a very stylish result.[2] The filmmaker confirmed:

> We had to be very faithful to Dudzinki's drawings, which he made using powdery, dry pastel on huge sheets of black paper. Initially, it seemed impossible to animate this pastel, until we started experimenting with some new methods. We also used computer animation for the

first time, but only for a few details. I enjoyed the fact that it was complex, but I hardly animated on this commercial; I was basically supervising.[1]

In the meantime, on 15 January 1989, Michael Dudok de Wit and Arielle Basset got married while travelling in India. They decided to continue living in London where they soon celebrated the arrival of their two children: Alexander, born in 1990, and Maya in 1992.

2.2 DISNEY MINDSET – *BEAUTY AND THE BEAST* (1989)

In 1989, Dudok de Wit took part in the European pre-production of Disney's *Beauty and the Beast* that was to be directed by Richard Purdum and produced by Don Hahn. The research, preliminary storyboards and story reel were planned at the Purdums' West End studio where several Disney animators flew in from California to join the European crew. The team worked incessantly, sometimes sixteen hours a day, for about three months in a row. Andreas Deja and Glen Keane animated; Tom Sito and Dudok de Wit did storyboards; Derek Gogol was in charge of product design and Jean Gilmore did the visual development. "I remember that I did not get to do any of the London sightseeing. We just worked like crazy and we delivered, in a very short space of time, a story reel in full colour, about 50 minutes long",[4] recalled Hans Bacher who is credited for colour, design and storyboard. Despite the incredible commitment of this strong team of top professionals, the European version of *Beauty and the Beast* came to a standstill. However Tom Sito reminisced about the problem with the story: "We had a very early treatment and the big songs hadn't gone in yet. The Disney producers weren't even sure if it was going to be a musical or not".[4]

After the screening of the story reel, Jeffrey Katzenberg, Disney's creative executive, decided to pull the plug on the pre-production in London. I think Dick Purdum had some creative differences with Katzenberg and the songwriters Howard Ashman and Alan Mencken on some of the early concepts. When the thing was going directly toward being a musical, perhaps it was going in a direction Dick didn't want to go in. So, Dick and Jill Thomas left the project and we all returned to L.A.,[6] concluded Tom Sito. Jill Thomas, on the other hand, has a rather more bitter recollection of events:

> When we were doing pre-production work on *Beauty and the Beast*, Michael worked on a section of the storyboard involving a chase sequence through a forest. The final cut of the Disney film uses much of the work he had done in our London studio, despite the fact that we had resigned from the production.[2]

Dudok de Wit learned a lot from his *Beauty and the Beast* experience. It was a well-paid job and

> socially very nice; we were all in the same large room. I tried to improve my skills by watching these veterans and I also tried to think in the Disney style. The Disney method of collaboration, a sort of weekly brainstorming session all together in front of our storyboard sections, was working efficiently from two points of view: firstly, we quickly identified the first weaknesses in each storyboard sequence and secondly, it created unity between the artists. Each of us tried to get approval from the others when we showed our work and, at the same time, we adjusted naturally to this unified mind – a Disney mindset. I found this totally fascinating.[1]

This London adventure made Dudok de Wit realise that he couldn't possibly be a Disney artist in the long run. Even though he respected the virtuosity and technical excellence of Disney's draughtsmen, as much as he admired their feel for movement and acting, he couldn't share their unconditional love for Disney's style of animation. However, he will later accept to freelance as an animator for Rob Minkoff's short film *Mickey's Audition* (1992) and Disney's feature *Fantasia 2000* (1999), but his Disney experience will conclude there.

After twelve years in commercial animation, the independent artist in Dudok de Wit started to feel restless, neglected and unsatisfied. He recognised that "being a commercial artist and entertainer was great on one level only. On a deeper level of my creativity, I yearned to move closer to the essence of things, somehow. The essence of pain, beauty, love and nature".[7] In his spare time, he worked on a storyboard about small Zen Buddhist monks who were sweeping a yard, for a short film based on *Winter*, the fourth concerto grosso from Antonio Vivaldi's *The Four Seasons*. He finally sent this non-narrative project, stylistically similar to his next short film, *The Monk and the Fish*, to Channel Four and the BBC, two of the largest British TV channels which frequently funded independent animated shorts. Unfortunately, both turned down the project, but Clare Kitson, the commissioner for Channel Four's animation, gave him one simple but illuminating piece of advice: "Think of a good, well developed story; people like good stories".[8]

2.3 *TOM SWEEP* (1992) – EASY, PURE AND JOYFUL ANIMATION

Another refusal resulted in a new disappointment, but Dudok de Wit's persevering nature always prevailed over the occasional professional frustrations, drawing yet more resolve from his latest misfortune. The short film project about the sweeping monks didn't work out, but maybe a small TV series, with short episodes, would be more compelling. It could also still look like a personal film: On such a small series I could be the main animator, writer and designer. The theme for *Tom Sweep* was cleaning the environment. The commercial value of the series would make it easier to find financial backing and it would be aimed at young audiences. The main character could even be used for merchandising ... At that time, TV series were not as lucrative as they are today, I think.[7] Dudok de Wit rapidly conceived the design and the storyline and tried his luck with the commercial market at the Annecy festival, but no one was interested. On his return to London, Jill Thomas and Richard Purdum offered to produce the pilot, and Dudok de Wit finished the film in twelve weeks: "I was fast with that easy, pure and joyful animation style and besides, several friends at the studio were helping me. I liked the pilot and I thought I was on the right track".[7]

Tom Sweep is a dialogue-free, two-minute pilot film about a little dustman who ceaselessly collects the garbage that other passers-by drop carelessly behind them on the street. The team used cel animation on watercolour backgrounds, and all was filmed in long shots. The characters were drawn directly on cel with watercolour brushes and black ink, a fairly unusual animation technique at that time.

The film is based on gags, repetitious melody defined by a playful accordion and snappy animation. Somehow it looks like a delicious homage to Charlie Chaplin's figure and humour that is reflected in Tom Sweep's comical body movements and clumsy little steps. The filmmaker's innate curiosity for the human body postures and movements is reflected in the variety of gaits of the other characters. Still the little restless dustman shares a significant visual resemblance with the agitated monk from his forthcoming film *The Monk and the Fish*: Tom's face is outlined with a thick or thin brush line with two dots instead of eyes. Dudok de Wit's brush line was inspired by the 17th century Japanese Zen Buddhist monks' paintings and calligraphy he had observed in a London exhibition back in 1981. *Tom Sweep*'s simple yellow-orange backgrounds in watercolour and the presence of thick shadows will take part in creating the atmosphere of *The Monk and the Fish*.

The filmmaker presented *Tom Sweep* at MIPCOM, an international film content market in Cannes, France. There he met an English producer, Iain Harvey, who seemed interested in submitting it to his Japanese contacts for the potential financing of the whole series.

> But sadly, Iain never found anyone. Moreover, Annecy festival didn't include the film in that year's selection ... That was disappointing and, for the second time, I had serious doubts whether to continue with animation. Years later, one French and one Spanish studio offered to finance the *Tom Sweep* series, but in both cases I considered it too risky, since I couldn't be there with the team.[1]

Dudok de Wit had already moved on: for him, *Tom Sweep* was history.

NOTES

1. Michael Dudok de Wit to Andrijana Ružić, London, 7 December 2018.
2. Jill Thomas's mail to Andrijana Ružić, 22 March 2019.
3. Wells, Paul, *Animation. Genre and Authorship*, Wallflower Press, London, 2002, p. 60.
4. Bacher, Hans, *Beauty and the Beast 1989*, *Animation Treasures*, 2 October 2009. https://one1more2time3.wordpress.com/2009/02/10/london-1989/, retrieved 17 December 2018.
5. Ghez, Didier, *Walt's People*, Volume 9, Interview with Tom Sito, Xlibris Corporation, Bloomington, 2010, p. 498.
6. Ghez, Didier, *Walt's People*, Volume 9, Interview with Tom Sito, Xlibris Corporation, Bloomington, 2010, p. 499.
7. Michael Dudok de Wit to Andrijana Ružić, London, 6 December 2018.
8. Kawa-Topor, Xavier, Nguyên, Ilan, *Michael Dudok de Wit. Le cinéma d'animation sensible. Entretien avec le réalisateur de La Tortue Rouge*, Capricci, Paris, 2019, p. 35. Translated from French by Andrijana Ružić.

CHAPTER 3

The Monk and the Fish (1994) – The Rise above Dualism

This heaven is so vast; no message can stain it.

TEN OX HERDING PICTURES, KAKUAN SHIEN,
ZEN BUDDHIST MONK, 12TH CENTURY

I N THE SUMMER OF 1993, an unexpected letter from the city of Valence in France arrived on Dudok de Wit's London address which will, quite unpredictably, change the course of his career.

The letter contained a brochure for an artists-in-residence programme from the studio Folimage and the timing couldn't have been better. All doubts and disillusions originating from a professional crisis Dudok de Wit went through in the previous years will be soothed in this French studio, founded in 1981 by Jacques-Rémy Girerd (1952), a visionary producer and animation director. Girerd's idea to move the axis of the French animation outside of Paris and its confusion, high living costs, competition and hectic lifestyle into the slow living and working pace of the city of Valence in south-eastern France proved to be a great success. Folimage has been focusing on the production of high-quality TV series for children and auteur's short films. Jayne Pilling has observed well that this scheme of reciprocal creative merging between the independent filmmakers in residence and the studio animators enriched immensely both sides. Especially Folimage studio animators, who benefited from filmmakers' new creative approaches and different techniques and have been stimulated to develop their own films in the meantime. This dismembering of the "job/skills demarcations with the clear advantages in terms of creative development"[1] made Folimage productions recognizable by their artisanal approach (hand-made 2D animation procrastinated to the end of the nineties) and graphic quality, in which artists' hands give vibrant textures to the visuals by means of chalk, pastels or paint.

Folimage studio started with the artists-in-residence programme in 1994, offering each year two young directors an opportunity to do a personal short animation film (up to seven minutes), without dialogues and with an authentic graphic style. The studio also provided professional assistance and their facilities in the period of six months. Dudok de Wit didn't think twice, and he applied to Folimage's competition. The old story about the sweeping monk he once sent to Clare Kitson at Channel Four seemed like a perfect idea for a further development. He recalled:

> I started thinking: I have a story with a monk in a monastery. I could rewrite the story, but this time it should be a film coming from an even deeper passion. To make a film that is entertaining and poetic at the same time, that's probably my highest potential. And if this doesn't work out, it will definitely confirm that I should leave the animation industry or focus on commercial animation only and be content with that.[2]

Not much time passed, and studio Folimage accepted his application: the filmmaker was enthusiastic about it, regaining in much needed self-confidence. Finally in January 1994, along with his wife Arielle and their two small children, Dudok de Wit left for France.

3.1 THE PLOT

A slim bell tower, a flock of birds in the summer sky, a row of cloister arcades, a long orange tile roof, a small fountain and an elongated aqueduct define the atmosphere of a Mediterranean Romanesque monastery. A monk in a brown robe appears on the edge of the cistern. Suddenly a small fish pops up of water in front of him. Determined to catch it, the monk returns to the monastery and fetches a fishing rod and a bucket. Jumping back and forth, he returns to the cistern and tries to catch the fish but falls into the water. Frustrated, he mimes several comical karate-like movements in the direction of the cistern. He then tries again, but with a fishing net this time – yet another failure. Long shadows and soft orange light introduce us to an afternoon hour in the monastery cell – the monk is trying to concentrate on a book. But he's restless and returns to reservoir accompanied by six fellow monks that jump around the water edge and suddenly leave. Dusky shadows dissolve into nighttime: a cloister, dormer windows, bell tower against a full moon, monastery courtyard is lined up with several cypresses and seven beds. All other monks are asleep except the restless one: he sneaks out into the monochrome night, armed with twelve candles. He lights them up along the cistern border and strikes the pose. Cut. Daylight, under the early sun, the monk is asleep, and candles are consumed. Cut. Armed with a long arch, with sharp choreographic movements, he fails to catch the fish again. Finally he decides to follow it and swims behind the fish across the aqueduct, passing through various landscapes: a row of cypresses, steep green rice pads, a group of terracotta amphoras, an intersection of two canals and the distant pyramids. In the final scene, the monk opens a huge door and lets the fish pass through. Fluctuating in the air both come out from a square window. Finally united, the serene monk and the fish dissolve in the distance, towards infinity.

3.2 CREATING AT THE STUDIO FOLIMAGE, FRANCE

The producer Jacques-Rémy Girerd suggested Dudok de Wit to anticipate his sojourn in France. He offered him to work for two months as an animator on the Folimage series *Ma petite planète chérie*, and the filmmaker accepted it. In the meantime, he familiarised with the studio team and the new environment. In the first months, Dudok de Wit realised that the studio Folimage was a perfect working place: its sense of community and a family atmosphere delighted him.

> The context was ideal: the whole animation team was working in the same room, on different projects, and in an amicable atmosphere. My film was progressing well and I felt supported. I was aligned with this project that I loved. For me it was a pure pleasure.[3]

The filmmaker will dedicate his remaining seven months' period to his new poetic film.

The Monk and the Fish was imagined as a story without dialogues (this will become the filmmaker's practice in all his future films) about the restlessness of a one-pointed monk and his obsession to catch an elusive fish. Reinforced by Arcangelo Corelli's version of *La Folìa*,[4] or even better embedded in its prodigious rhythm, the essence of *The Monk and the Fish* is in its ending: in the final union of the two protagonists. The story is based on an ancient Taoist legend about an ox and an oxherd, revised by a Chinese monk Kakuan Shien in the 12th century. Shien also created ten images with accompanying verses that explain the most salient points of the practice on the path of enlightenment at which Zen Buddhism aims. The monk in Dudok de Wit's film could easily be identified with the oxherd, whereas the fish could stand for the ox, although the film doesn't go as far as the Chinese pictures "because of the ten pictures, the final four were so profound that I couldn't reproduce them with my own authority",[5] said Dudok de Wit. Instead he had chosen to let himself be inspired by the idea of "the ox and oxherd separate in the beginning but united in the realization of the inner unity of all existence".[6] For the filmmaker, this part was of an utmost importance, he even conceived the whole film starting from its poetic ending, the final serene union after one long, agitated separation.

Says the director:

> The problem was that this ending by itself would have been flat, too boring or too mysterious to pull the audience in, so I clearly needed to have a build-up of the story, to establish a minimum of empathy towards the monk character.[2]

This necessary build-up was the introduction of the "archetypal motif of the pursuit"[7] into this spiritual story. Dudok de Wit managed to seduce the spectator's attention by simply making the film entertaining and funny, with the little gags based on the variations of repetitions of unsuccessful monk's catching of the fish that also create a bit of suspense. In contrast to the ending, in the beginning the monk is obsessed, but he finally arrives at a resolution in a quiet way. "The real purpose of my film is its ending. If it wasn't for that ending, I wouldn't have made the film",[7] said the filmmaker.

The visually clear storyboard of *The Monk and the Fish* consisted of simple cartoony images drawn in graphite and accompanied by one or two short descriptive phrases. The director has taken out from his previous project only the design of the monk (but he slightly changed the shape of his tunic) and the location, a clearly Mediterranean setting of a Romanesque monastery.[8] The row of dark cypresses and their long shadows, reflected in the water, anticipate the typical row of poplars near the canals and Dutch polders that will be the setting for his next film, *Father and Daughter* (2000).

Dudok de Wit decided to create the film images with the combination of two traditional liquid techniques: black ink and watercolour. Benefitting from the experience with these painting techniques, forged in TV commercials and in short pilot *Tom Sweep*, the filmmaker drew the characters directly on cel by using watercolour brushes and black ink and coloured them with acrylic colours on the back. The ink line varied in thickness depending on the purpose – thicker for the shadows and finer for the character's features. The backgrounds were done with loose strokes on the watercolour paper, although the background lines were painted on their own layer of cel. They are bright and seem lit underneath. In this way, Dudok de Wit created a pleasantly tactile contrast between the sharp, black ink line, granular and vaporous watercolour paper and the loose strokes of watercolour paint that didn't fill in evenly the borders of the black outlining.[9]

The ink paintings of Zen Buddhist monks that he had seen in 1980 at the London Great Japan Exhibition will become the filmmaker's constant inspiration in his future work. He noticed in these artworks all the qualities that define his own ideal of a visual perfection: "the simplicity, the elegance of the line, the sensitivity to empty space and the use of the brush".[10] He was particularly impressed by the way artists from the Far East consciously used empty space in their art, and he was inspired to explore the presence of empty space in his own work.

Nevertheless, all these inspirational Eastern graphic visuals remained a reverberation in his artwork, a sort of a slight indication of the existence of that far away, mysterious world he felt so much attracted to.

Japanese animation director Isao Takahata (1935–2018) accordingly observed that

> *The Ten Oxherd* images are very much studied by Westerners who consider it a very accomplished artistic form. I am not convinced … I did not perceive this inclination towards the East in *The Monk and the Fish*.

The Japanese are primarily looking for impetus of the line, whilst Michael is working on the perception of volume through the shadows. He searches for the light by using shadows.[11]

And effectively, the abundancy of form and cast shadows, other characteristics of Dudok de Wit's visual aesthetics, coalesced into the protagonist's reflections on the water surface. The shapes of the shadows, combined with the general colours of the scene, indicate the time of the day, while the character's reflections on the opaque water surface introduce the beauty of synchronisation.

"The reflections in the water were important too, they added an extra quality. I will give you an example: if you see a dancer on stage, dancing alone, you probably enjoy the sight. If you see two people dancing in synchronization, this can be even more attractive, because synchronization by itself is beautiful. If you see a character in a film moving around, and this character's movements are clearly reflected on a smooth water surface, like that of a pond, the perfect synchronization may create a subtle pleasure. Even when you don't look directly at the reflection, you feel it. This adds a little extra appeal to the scene and besides, it can also create a unique ambience",[12] explained Dudok de Wit.

As a question of taste for simplicity and certain colour predilections, there is an extremely limited gamut of colours in this film: brown and ocher, ultramarine blue and indigo. The director also added a small amount of red colour, almost imperceptible, in the decisive moment of the film where the monk stops chasing the fish:

> I find subtle colors interesting, for example on days when the sky is grey. There's also great beauty in black and white cinema and photography, and in monochrome paintings with a subtle use of two colors. In *The Monk and the Fish* I used two basic colors, variations of yellow-brown and variations of blue. That's a graceful color combination and not excessively warm.[2]

The predilection for round forms (semicircular arches and windows, rice paddies' contours, the shape of the monk's head, even the filmmaker's handwriting that appears in the opening and closing titles) is defined by the filmmaker as an unconscious motif and aesthetical attraction: "For me, the arch and the circle are motifs which belong to the construction of my films, not only pictorially but also narratively".[13]

Like in *Tom Sweep*, the whole film is made in long shots without close-ups whatsoever. The monk is always shown in the distance, well integrated into his universe. If we could zoom in his face, we would realise that he has two dots for the eyes and one for the nose. His emotional state is conveyed rather through his body language, where the application of the principle of squash and stretch results in the vigorous snappiness of his movements, through the soundtrack and the general atmosphere of the film. Everything we have to know about the monk is that there is something very pure and simple about him.

> The monk hasn't got a complicated life: he lives most of his life in one place, and he probably spends a lot of time alone. When I want him to be excited, he moves his arms, and when he's really intense, the animation becomes faster and his body language becomes wilder.[14]

Following the linear storytelling, the editing is softened by gradual transitions from one image to another, in which scenes overlap transporting us smoothly to the next sequences and locations. Thus, the editing appears seamless, which is partly a result of filmmaker's experimenting with cross dissolves and partly because of the way he uses the film language. "In addition", explained Dudok de Wit, the editing may seem fluid due to the consistent right–left orientation (the monk goes towards the right when he approaches the water reservoir, and he moves towards the left when he leaves) and to the tight relationship between the visuals and the music.[15]

3.3 ANIMATION – A CHOREOGRAPHY OF RESTLESSNESS

The expressive force and vitality of the main character lies in a singular dualism of his contradictory character. The poor monk doesn't have a peace of mind: he's obsessed. His exasperated body will be quietened down only in the final scene of a peaceful union with the fish. This particular trait of monk's restlessness reflects itself in the state of mind of the filmmaker in that moment of his life:

> In those years there was a monk in me that was looking for purity, simplicity and spirituality. It was not a coincidence that I drew this character. Part of me was a monk: not typically Christian, maybe more Buddhist or something else, but a monk for sure.[16]

The Monk and the Fish was done in the traditional animation and that means with the pencil and paper on the lightbox. Dudok de Wit would test the movements of the characters by a line test and would correct the animation if something didn't work. In the next phase, he would put a cel on top of the right drawing and would copy it with the brush.

In the beginning, he was mainly animating alone, but towards the end of the production, he felt the need for an additional back-up. At that point, the studio Folimage proposed a Canadian animator, Guy Delisle (1966), who had been previously working in TV series and whose simple and fresh animation in a short film *Trois Petit Chats* was appreciated by Dudok de Wit. In the end, Delisle has been offered an opportunity to co-animate on the project for additional three months. Today a well-known author of graphic novels, Delisle described Dudok de Wit's unique style of animation:

> I've never worked on a film like that before: Michael was directly inking some scenes on the cels! It was the most interesting job I got in my ten years of animation.[17]

Dudok de Wit was experienced in different styles of animation and about the effects one could create with a particular
brush or a particular execution speed. In *The Monk and the Fish*,
the solidity of the line was the director's aesthetic choice, and the
thickness of the line varied a lot because the brush has the tendency to float on the surface. Dudok de Wit explained:

> The watercolour brush is a very sensitive tool and the
> smallest vibration in your hand is magnified in the line.
> Mistakes are complicated to fix. But if your animation
> is fast and snappy, you don't have that problem as much.
> I wanted the monk's movements to be snappy, because
> it was fun to animate and to watch and it corresponded
> well with the lively music. In that animation style draw-
> ings change a lot from frame to frame and you use fewer
> in-between drawings. This is tricky and you have to
> keep checking that the overall movement is smooth and
> clear.[2]

Animation historian Giannalberto Bendazzi observed well that
Dudok de Wit has "a special talent for creating a movement. In
The Monk and the Fish the main character acts and gesticulates
in an expressive staccato style not seen before".[18] This sparkling
quality of Dudok de Wit's animation, which was very present in
Tom Sweep as well, is the result of filmmaker's mastering over
time efficiency. Moreover the director in this short pays also
another homage to Chaplin's oeuvre and more specifically to his
sense of humour imbued in the monk's comic body language.
Finally, it's all about that mysterious animation ingredient called
timing that will define Dudok de Wit's characteristic animation
style.

3.4 *LA FOLÌA* – THE IMPETUS OF THE PURSUIT

Dudok de Wit heard *La Folìa* on the radio back in his student
days and immediately thought that it would be an excellent
musical accompaniment to a short film. Later on he discovered

various composers, who had adapted this traditional Renaissance musical theme in their compositions, such as Alessandro Scarlatti, Francesco Geminiani, Antonio Vivaldi, Arcangelo Corelli, Georg Friedrich Haendl, J. S. Bach and Antonio Salieri.

La Folìa with its various range of emotions worked well for Dudok de Wit's story, because it consisted of one melody repeated over and over again. He needed these musical repetitions in order to fit them into narration and diversify the unsuccessful monk's attempts to catch the fish by turning them into funny gags. The filmmaker knows well that there's something very powerful about the repetition in animation:

> Whenever you animate a movement, even if it is just one second long, you film the line drawings to test the quality of the movement. You look at the line test a few times, maybe even dozens of times, on a loop. And when you do that, something bizarre happens: this repetition of the same movement has a subtle hypnotic effect on you. This kind of repetition and other kinds of repetition are popular in animation and if the filmmaker uses them well, the spectator will be entertained by them.[2]

A good example of this reasoning is the sequence where the monk uses a bow and arrow to catch the fish. There is a lot of repetition in the monk's agitation, and it stops abruptly when monk finishes in the pond. Music and animation, by feeding each other, result in total symbiosis here.

Dudok de Wit originally drew a storyboard with *La Folìa* in mind and measured accurately all the musical segments. He then chose the recordings of *La Folìa* versions he liked the most, for example, the Corelli's one. Everything was ready; only the composer was missing.

At that point, studio Folimage presented their regular collaborator, the French composer Serge Besset, to the filmmaker. Besset was very experienced in composing for animated films, and he knew very well the working methods of animators and how precise, meticulous and controlling they can be. Dudok de Wit remembers Besset as "a very humble person, very intuitive, wonderful. We instantly became friends".[19] He gave the composer indications of the music, of emotions and of the length of every chapter of the music. He pointed out on the storyboard which part was to be slow or where was a gap for a transition. He passed him little sketches in which he explained how to split all the different parts of his music over the film. The composer understood immediately the snappiness of the monk's movements.

Here's how Besset remembers the time of this collaboration:

> The animatic didn't exist and Michael had all the film in his head, frame by frame, with a very precise timing. In the beginning I had only the storyboard on disposal and some very precise indications. And at the end I was locked up in them. I've never worked like this before! For *The Monk and the Fish* it took me around 3 months to adapt my music to Michael's indications, second by second, and transcript them into my music. There were fourteen parts with different tempos and they were very important since they had to adapt the music to the film. My biggest challenge was how to adapt my music to Michael's timing.[20]

After the first month of production, Besset did a music on a sampler with the imitation sound of instruments. Once this work was finished, Dudok de Wit used it for a timing guide for animation. He analysed the music with its actions and silences; he made a lot of technical notes and used them very accurately for the animation. When all the animation was finished and coloured, they went back to Besset's music studio, and they recorded the music with live instruments: viola da gamba, cello, oboe, flute, guitar, trumpets.

In *The Monk and the Fish*, which is a film without dialogues and with a minimum of sound effects (only the sounds of birds and water from a small fountain), music becomes everything because its whole visuals are structured on it. In this case, the synchronization also had to be very strong because the music in certain moments was replacing the sound effects as well.

This triplet of repetitions (musical variations, narrative repetitions, repetitions in animation) in the film's consequent vitality enchanted a lot of animators and animation directors,[21] but Barry J. C. Purves[22] offered the most convincing explanation of his enthusiasm for this film that often left him "dewy eyed":

> One of the most beautiful marriages of movement, rhythm and music has to be Michael Dudok de Wit's exquisite *The Monk and the Fish*, set to music by Corelli. It is hard to imagine one without the other. The music adds joy and life and makes the film flow. Usually classical orchestral sounds need a suitable richness from the visuals to work, but here the drawings are simple and the music is appropriate.[23]

3.5 SYMBOLISMS, METAPHORS AND MESSAGES

I cannot think of another animation film author who has treated abstract and spiritual concepts with such vitality, lightheartedness, formal elegance and humour.[24] All the components of the film language are in harmony here: Besset's musical variations on Corelli's *La Folia* are perfectly woven into a sparky animation, monk's convincing acting in the soothed atmosphere of the warm Mediterranean backgrounds and the incisiveness of the black ink brush line over a harmonious and parsimonious colour palette.

In this film, Dudok de Wit's European cultural roots (Western European classical music, architectural set, linear perspective, homage to Chaplin's humour) meet one Far Eastern legend and thus formulate the film's universal message. This specific marriage of European and Oriental motifs in *The Monk and the Fish*, these two completely different sources of inspiration, will become typical of Dudok de Wit's film poetics and his creative universe.

The Japanese animation director Isao Takahata enthusiastically commented: "I loved it at first sight. Everything – the drawing, animation, music, story and sense of humor – was magnificent. I fell in love with it. I was especially astonished by its powerful sense of reality, despite its simplicity".[25]

Still the film's simple and yet ingenuous visuals serve as a build-up for some serious, spiritual content. *The Monk and the Fish* transmits the feeling of joyous liberation, it's a celebration-of-life film in a way. It makes us reflect about the ways of addressing the obstacles and adversities in life and maybe to accept rather than oppose them. It shows us that it is better perhaps to accept our limits by trying to overcome them.

The filmmaker commented[26] *The Monk and the Fish* as the film about the protagonist's one-pointedness and monomania[27]: the monk wants only one thing, the fish, and that is what it symbolises. That's the most important thing, everything else is secondary.

But he also left a large margin of liberty of interpretation to his public which depends on diverse individual sensibilities: for an artist, the film could symbolise the quest for the perfection in his/her art; for a mystic, it could mean searching for a perfection in spirituality; for someone who wants a happy family, it could signify a perfect domestic happiness.

> It was my ambition to make a film that could act as a mirror, on the surface of which people could see a reflection of their inner lives. Many storytellers have this ambition, but when you think about it, it's quite an astonishing ambition. Is it arrogant? I think it is neither arrogant nor humble. It is how we deal with it that makes it arrogant or not. I feel a huge respect for this ambition.[28]

The presence of three natural elements, earth, water and air, could have another symbolical significance. The director recounted that

> some spectators have noted that each character is attached to its element: the monk is on the ground and

the fish is in the water. They need a third element, the air, to find themselves. For me it is about transcendence which makes union possible.[29]

But he also pointed out that he didn't want to make a film with a message that is specifically Christian in spite of the fact that in the film are present certain elements of Christian iconography.[30]

Still, if you're a Christian and you see a Christian message, perfect. If you're an atheist and you see a story about two characters, that's perfect too. *The Monk and the Fish* is not a story about the solution of a conflict, it's more about the rise above a conflict, the rise above duality. The monk doesn't get the fish by using cleverness, force or any other means. The story doesn't tell us how to catch a fish. But if some spectators find that the film resonates with them on an intuitive level, I'm delighted. Meanwhile, for me personally, the film metaphorically conveys spirituality: it is about the simple yet extraordinary realization of union, or unity, when somehow, mysteriously, everything falls into place. During those years I had intimations of this unity and they were strong. I felt ready to express, in a symbolic way, the notion of unity in a film,[2] concluded the filmmaker.

The film immediately started travelling worldwide, just like its serene protagonist in the last sequence when he rose above his local environment by passing through different landscapes. With such a poetic and spiritual film, Dudok de Wit was eager to know whether he succeeded to communicate with the spectators.[31] The awards that started coming in very soon confirmed his hopes: the first one came from the animation festival in Espinho, Portugal, followed by the others from France (César,[32] Annecy), Canada (Ottawa), Japan (Hiroshima). The film was even nominated for the Academy Award for the Best Animated Short Film. Dudok de Wit was overwhelmed: after fifteen years in the animation industry, he received public recognition for his artistic achievements. At this point, he already started dreaming about a new film.

NOTES

1. Pilling, Jayne, *2D and Beyond*, RotoVision SA, Switzerland, 2001, p. 140.

2. Michael Dudok de Wit to Andrijana Ružić, London, 6 December 2018.

3. Kawa-Topor, Xavier, Nguyên, Ilan, *Michael Dudok de Wit. Le cinéma d'animation sensible. Entretien avec le réalisa-teur de La Tortue Rouge*, Capricci, Paris, 2019, p. 40. Translated from French by Andrijana Ružić.

4. *La Follia* (ital.) or *La Folìa* (Port.) is an ancient melody developed out of the folk music in Portugal of the late 15th century. Its popularity spread from Spain to almost all Mediterranean countries. In the Baroque period, *La Folìa* slowed down on a particular melody, becoming more elegant and graceful. The adaptability of *La Folìa* and the variations of its melody were the reasons of its enormous popularity that lasted throughout 18th century. See Valentino, Andrea, *Could La Folìa be history's most enduring tune?* BBC Culture, 31 July 2019, http://www.bbc.com/culture/story/20190726-could-la-folia-be-historys-most-enduring-tune, retrieved 6 September 2019.

5. Molinhoff, Sara, *A Beautiful Language*, The Oxonian Review, 11 May 2009, http://www.oxonianreview.org/wp/a-beautiful-language/, retrieved 7 May 2019.

6. Koller, M. John, *Ox herding: Stages of Zen Practice*, http://www.columbia.edu/cu/weai/exeas/resources/pdf/oxherding.pdf, retrieved on 11 May 2019.

7. Kawa-Topor, Xavier, Nguyên, Ilan, Michael Dudok de Wit. *Le cinéma d'animation sensible. Entretien avec le réalisa-teur de La Tortue Rouge*, Capricci, Paris, 2019, p. 48.

8. "I wanted a very pure Romanesque architecture in the film, with very few decorations. I have always been fascinated by modest Romanesque buildings with harmonious proportions". In Kawa-Topor, Xavier, Nguyên, Ilan, *Michael Dudok de Wit. Le cinéma d'animation sensible. Entretien avec le réalisa-teur de La Tortue Rouge*, Capricci, Paris, 2019, p. 41.

9. For detailed information about techniques and tools see Furniss, Maureen, *The Animation Bible*, Abrams, New York, 2008, p. 211.

10. Kawa-Topor, Xavier, Nguyên, Ilan, *Michael Dudok de Wit. Le cinéma d'animation sensible. Entretien avec le réalisa-teur de La Tortue Rouge*, Capricci, Paris, 2019, p. 166.

11. Dreyfus, Stéphane, *Takahata – Dudok de Wit: Rencontre au sommet*, 25 November 2016, https://film-animation.blogs.la-croix.com/takahata-dudok-de-wit-rencontre-au-sommet/2016/11/25/, retrieved 6 May 2019.
12. Michael Dudok de Wit to Andrijana Ružić, Zagreb, 9 June 2017.
13. Kawa-Topor, Xavier, Nguyên, Ilan, Michael *Dudok de Wit. Le cinéma d'animation sensible. Entretien avec le réalisa-teur de La Tortue Rouge*, Capricci, Paris, 2019, p. 45.
14. Michael Dudok de Wit in Teachers TV: Reading a film *The Monk and the Fish*, https://www.youtube.com/watch?v=s9dHJro69f4, retrieved 26 February 2019.
15. Michael Dudok de Wit's email to Andrijana Ružić, 2 January 2020.
16. Kawa-Topor, Xavier, Nguyên, Ilan, *Michael Dudok de Wit. Le cinéma d'animation sensible. Entretien avec le réalisa-teur de La Tortue Rouge*, Capricci, Paris, 2019, p. 41.
17. Guy Delisle's email to Andrijana Ružić, 19 September 2017.
18. Bendazzi, Giannalberto, *Animation: A World History: Volume III*, CRC Press, Routledge, 2016, p. 115.
19. Michael Dudok de Wit to Andrijana Ružić, Interview on Mirogoj cemetery, Zagreb, Croatia, 9 June 2017.
20. Serge Besset's email to Andrijana Ružić, 19 January 2019.
21. See the Appendix *Critical Reception of Michael Dudok de Wit's Films*.
22. Barry J. C. Purves (1955) is an English animator director and writer of puppet animation films and theatre designer and director.
23. Purves, Barry J. C., *Stop Motion: Passion, Process and Performance*, Focal Press, New York and London, 2007, p. 283
24. Maybe only New York director and animator Faith Hubley (1924–2001) had a similar vital approach to spiritual topics in her short avant-garde films, but she'd usually addressed them without wit.
25. *Interview with Isao Takahata*, Press Kit, Wild Bunch International Sales, https://www.wildbunch.biz/movie/the-red-turtle/, last retrieved 2 February 2018.
26. Michael Dudok de Wit to Andrijana Ružić, Interview on Mirogoj cemetery, Zagreb, Croatia, 9 June 2017.
27. Kawa-Topor, Xavier, Nguyên, Ilan, *Michael Dudok de Wit. Le cinéma d'animation sensible. Entretien avec le réalisa-teur de La Tortue Rouge*, Capricci, Paris, 2019, p. 49.

28. Michael Dudok de Wit's mail to Andrijana Ružić, 31 December 2019.
29. Kawa-Topor, Xavier, Nguyên, Ilan, *Michael Dudok de Wit. Le cinéma d'animation sensible. Entretien avec le réalisa-teur de La Tortue Rouge*, Capricci, Paris, 2019, p. 163.
30. The fish as a symbol of Christ, the Christian monastic setting.
31. "When my film won the César award in the Best Short Film Category, I was very pleased and it was also a distinct ego boost. The career artist in me wanted people to applaud my project". Michael Dudok de Wit to Andrijana Ružić, London, 6 December 2018.
32. César Award is the national film award of France established in 1976.

CHAPTER 4

Father and Daughter (2000) – Biography of Longing

Yama-san said: "Kurosawa, this sequence is not drama. It's *mono-no-aware*". Mono-no-aware, "sadness at the fleeting nature of things", like the sweet, nostalgic sorrow of watching the cherry blossoms fall – when I heard this ancient poetic term, I was suddenly struck by enlightenment as if waking from a dream. "I understand!" I exclaimed and set about completely re-editing the scene. I put together only the long shots.[1]

AKIRA KUROSAWA

WHO WOULD HAVE THOUGHT that a short film about a life-long longing of a daughter for an absent father would become the most rewarded one on all the most important international festivals of animation in the period from 2000 to 2004? Michael Dudok de Wit was the first one that nurtured doubts about the film's reception: he felt that the specificity of a local, Dutch setting, the lyrical, almost humourless and overall melancholic quality of *Father and Daughter* would probably have a very restricted audience.[2] However, his doubts were proved to be wrong – the audience all over the world loved it from its very first public screening.

4.1   THE PLOT

Father and daughter ride their bicycles along a dike in the midst of imaginary Dutch polders.[3] They stop beside a pair of high poplar trees and say goodbye. Father starts descending the dike towards the small boat in the water. Suddenly he returns to the little girl, takes her in his arms, they shortly twirl around in a strong embrace. Father then redescends to the boat and starts rowing towards the horizon. On the golden eve, near the poplars, the little girl excitedly jumps back and forth looking in the direction of the horizon. The sun goes down, but her father doesn't come back. While seasons unfold and years go by, the daughter evolves as well: we see her as a child, adolescent, young woman and finally the mother of two children. With a gritty determination, she keeps returning to the place where her father left off. Over the years, the landscape transforms, the water drains off the land, the daughter becomes an old woman. Life has given her a lot; only her father didn't return.[4] In the final scene, she slowly pushes her bicycle and stops by the pair of poplar trees. She descends the dike and enters a vast field covered with high grass.[5] She comes across an abandoned rowboat, similar to that of her father, stuck in the dry mud. She touches the boat, enters inside, lies down on her side and seemingly falls asleep. Suddenly she awakes and feels that something has changed. She stands up, starts to walk and then to run, with each step becoming younger. Incredulous, she stops in front of her father, gets one step closer. They look at each other for a short moment. Finally, solaced by a strong embrace, their sharp elongated shadows become one.

4.2   A TUMULTUOUS BEGINNING

Fortified by the overall positive worldwide reception of *The Monk and the Fish*, Dudok de Wit was enthused about his new personal film: he already had a storyboard and a British producer Claire Jennings, but he was hesitating. He felt that a new story, with a Greek philosopher as a main character, was not ready yet. It was in 1996, and he was teaching animation at the National Film and TV School, not far from London. At the school library, he came upon several short, monochrome films, in sepia and white and black and white colour by the Polish animation director Piotr Dumała.[6] Dudok de Wit was especially fascinated by monochrome and poetic quality of two Dumała's short films, *Łagodna* (1985) and *Franz Kafka* (1991), in which the Polish filmmaker's original technique of engraved plasterboard produced masterful results in oneiric and dark visions shaped by the silence, light and chiaroscuro effects.

Later that day, while driving home, with rarefied and melancholic atmospheres from Dumała's films in mind, he asked himself one simple question: What do I want to express most in my personal film? And the answer came very clearly: I want to express the feeling of longing. A very deep, quiet longing that can in a subtle way be present in us during our whole life.[2] He later described more precisely this particular sentiment as the one that is lived in a pure and conscious way. And even if this deep desire is a form of suffering, the purity of this suffering is honest; I would even say that it is noble. There, I felt, was material for a film that would touch me deeply.[7]

In that precise moment of illumination, the whole story, incisive and vivid, unrolled in his mind: his film is going to tell a story about a separation of a father and daughter and her lifelong yearning in his absence, followed by their final union. The filmmaker immediately informed the producer Claire Jennings about the new idea for a film. In the meantime, he thought to involve the Dutch producers as well into the project: he approached Nico Crama, one of the most successful animation producers in the

Netherlands. But Crama, who was about to retire in that year, offered his colleague Willem Thijssen to take over Dudok de Wit's project. Thijssen accepted the offer, and in 1996 his production company CinéTé immediately addressed the Dutch Film Fund and got the financial support for the initial development of the film. Thijssen also managed to obtain a financial support from the local VPRO broadcaster.

"They all agreed almost right away, everyone loved Michael's project. I saw the storyboard almost 'being born'. It was such a great idea from the very beginning: the setting was very Dutch, but the theme was universal. Michael was open for all kind of discussions, so I suggested to him to change the film title to *Waterloos* (Dutch meaning 'without water'). Nevertheless he liked more his own choice and the title *Father and Daughter* remained definitive",[8] recalled Thijssen.

Finally, the film was set up as an international co-production. Thijssen oversaw the initial investment of 50% of the budget, which covered the storyboard development, while the rest of the finance was to be secured by the production company Cloudrunner Ltd, run by Claire Jennings. She managed to enter into an agreement with the British Film Fund, while Channel Four accepted to broadcast the film in the UK. The contribution from the National Lottery was also planned. Unfortunately the British producer encountered some serious fundraising problems, and when the National Lottery finally provided the rest of 30% of funds, Channel Four took a step back. There was a conspicuous hole in the budget on the British side, and at that point, Dudok de Wit did what he usually never does: he decided to start anyway.

> It was risky to start animating because of the chance that the film would never receive proper funding and that it would therefore not be made, or it would be made incredibly slowly during my weekends and free days. But I strongly believed in the film on a personal level, in other words, I knew that the film would be aligned with

my creative integrity – which by the way is the best feeling an artist can aim for – and on a practical level, that the film, even though there was little humour, would have a story that could possibly work for Dutch audiences and maybe non-Dutch audiences too. I thought somehow naively that there would be a financial solution, that money would come later from Channel Four, for example. But that didn't happen.[2]

Exactly at that time, he was invited to teach at the Art School in Kassel, Germany, where he replaced animation director Paul Driessen, who went on his sabbatical leave. The only possible solution at that point was to continue to work on the film by stopping on a regular basis to teach in Kassel where he had been lecturing for two years. In this way, he was able to finance his own filmmaker's fee only to see his film finished after four years of discontinuous work.

4.3   FROM STORYTELLING TO STORYBOARD

"In my films the ideas just come up, the symbols come up, the emotions come up. I start with really fine emotions including serenity, if one could call that an emotion. Then come the images, the symbols and the rational thinking that I use to structure everything",[9] explicated the filmmaker.

It somehow seems that Dudok de Wit has the tendency to put the protagonists of his films in front of the strongest temptations in life as if he wants to test their resistance. In his previous short film *The Monk and the Fish*, he exasperated both mind and body of the main character during his memorable quest to catch the fish. In *Father and Daughter*, he challenged the perseverance of the protagonist by alternating obstacles and anticipations during her constant lifelong yearning. But how was he supposed to symbolically transpose the presence of such a feeling into a film? The filmmaker intuitively felt that an archetypal event of a father and daughter's separation seemed strong enough to convey the desired intensity of this strong sentiment.[10]

Dudok de Wit divided his dialogue-free story into ten chapters which recount the most significant lifespan stages of a fatherless daughter. With this reasoning, the idea of separation and union becomes the backbone of the storyline, with the opening farewell scene and the final reunion scene as the ones with major emotional density. The sense of passing of time is accentuated by several recurring motifs: the rotating of bicycle wheels and the changing of seasons, with consequential metamorphosis of the landscape as well as the daughter's gradual ageing. There are no reminiscences, and the time unfolds inexorably towards the daughter's future. We don't know the reason for their separation; we don't know anything about their past. We haven't seen their home, or other components of the family. Instead the filmmaker decided to concentrate his attention exclusively, and with a very serene pacing, on daughter's yearning as a consequence of father's absence. More precisely, the filmmaker's intention was to visually express the notion of separation followed by union during "the creative process that involved a lot of simplification".[11]

The additional characters, the passersby on bicycles, are another constituting element of the life cycle: they are all females,[12] and regarding of their age, they are distinguished with the variety of clothing and body postures. Every single person that appears on the dike is important for the storytelling structure: in the windy day chapter (2:41), a little daughter encounters an old woman, covered with a heavy woollen shawl and pushing her bicycle against the strong wind. This woman is the mirror image of the aged daughter that appears in the two final chapters. In the ninth chapter (5:21), we see an aged daughter with a precarious balance on the bike, encountering a young girl that has the same age as herself in first scene of the film. In the tenth chapter (6:08), the protagonist is an old, tired lady, who pushes slowly her bicycle for the last time and stumbles upon a child on the dike, cycling in the opposite direction. In this manner, the narrative structure embraces the entire daughter's life cycle reverberated in the life cycles of the additional characters.

There appears to be one structural incoherence in the storyline though: in the final union scene, the filmmaker chose to represent the daughter as a young adult, not as a five-year-old from the initial, farewell scene. The filmmaker explained that originally his decision was purely intuitive, only to realise later that the young adult would be mature enough to digest the separation and to have a better understanding of her own emotions. As much as our body has a physical age, on a deeper level we know that we are ageless. We are always of the same, timeless essence. So if we were to choose our physical identity, in the ending of this particular story, we would possibly choose an age in which we are in good health, still young but adult and with a future ahead.[13]

With the finalised story development, Dudok de Wit made the first sketches with black and brown 2B and 3B pencils in which the hatchings create very fine shading effects, thus creating a specific mood and the quality of light. In all this, the filmmaker was inspired by "the magnificent sky"[14] represented in Rembrandt's etching *The Three Trees* whose copy was hanging on the wall of his childhood bedroom. But the first rough sketches were also based on his own memories of Dutch landscapes he used to explore as a child on a bicycle and "the beauty of the polder, which reaches far into the distance, into infinity".[15]

In the next visual stage, the filmmaker had to define the design of the characters and the landscape which included a lot of research: reference images and videos of cyclists and birds, clouds, landscapes, boats, trees, period clothing, in order to distil all the visual information into a simple selection.[16] He visited Holland a couple of times in order to have objective references before his eyes and see how a child, an adolescent or an elderly person gets on or off their bicycles. Willem Thijssen, the co-producer of *Father and Daughter*, informed me that the Dutch people cycle in a different way than the British,[17] which was also confirmed by Dudok de Wit:

The Dutch, both young and old, cycle side by side in a social way and even today helmets are not worn in the Netherlands. The cyclists' postures are unique; they look like they're sitting on a chair, in an upright position. That's because Dutch bicycles are large; they have big wheels and high handlebars. There's something inviting about this upright position and I wanted to convey this inviting posture in my film.[2]

The most important part of the pre-production phase, however, was the composition of the storyboard in which the filmmaker sought for utter simplification of each component of the film. Generally speaking Dudok de Wit's working method is based on carefully elaborated storyboards which he later uses as a firm reference for animation and timing. The storyboarding lasted several months due to a large number of drawings and the necessary time to think about the narrative flow and overall structural coherence. The storyboard consisted of about a hundred and sixty pictures which were drawn with soft black pencil on animation paper:

I sketch about six to eight individual simple drawings in one go, cut them out, lay them in sequence on the table, experiment a little with their chronological order, maybe add some extra drawings. After this I sketch the next lot of pictures. Eventually the whole story lies exposed on the table or on the floor and I keep rearranging the drawings until the story and the visuals feel right. I then redraw everything and I add the storyboard text. Before I start animating, I hang all storyboard pictures in sequence on the wall and leave them there until the end of production.[18]

Experimenting with new techniques has always been Dudok de Wit's pleasure. In his previous films, he had explored rich and vapourous possibilities of representing light and shadows in watercolours, but this technique didn't seem right for the mood he wanted to express in his new film. Out of curiosity, he did his first sketch with charcoal which he hadn't used since his student days at the Geneva Academy of Fine Arts. He liked the hand-made look of charcoal and instantly thought that it was a fast and intuitive tool with an appropriate texture and materiality that fully engages the artistic gesture and its physical, bodily dimension. I believe in the intelligence of the body that expresses intuition in a better way. It's like in dancing: when you dance, certain parts of your body are invisible to you, but you feel that the beauty is there, in the movements. It is extremely important for me to use my hands when I draw. It nourishes me,[19] explained the filmmaker. With the emulation of the transparent quality of watercolour, the film achieved a slightly painterly look.[20] The backgrounds were done with charcoal and pencil on a grainy animation paper with a typical artisanal method: the sky and the clouds were drawn by smudging the charcoal surface with fingertips (for clouds) or with the palm of a hand (sky).

Very early in the process, the filmmaker had to decide about the choice of colours. He originally intended to use green because it is the colour of Dutch landscapes, polders and fields, extending up to the horizon – but it didn't convince him. He tried then with brown and sepia colour and carefully selected hues of sepia, brown and blue which seemed appropriate for the prevailing nostalgic atmosphere. The colours were indicated in the colour model together with all the necessary textures that enriched the final visual effect. The choice to give to the main character faint blue garments was made for the graphic reasons:

> Sepia colour with just a little touch of blue looked very nice. Another practical reason was: she aged dramatically throughout the film and therefore changed design a lot. By giving her always the same bluish colours, it would hopefully be smoother for the spectator to totally stay with her (I did the same with Tom Sweep, who was the only one with blue garments in the film).[21]

The inspiration for the settings derived from different reference materials, in particular from a series of black and white photography books of Dutch landscapes belonging to his father's family library and from the distillation of filmmaker's own childhood memories from Holland. An almost monochrome Dutch landscape (flat and desolate plain fields, vast horizons, polders and poplar trees), gradually transformed throughout the years, can be seen as another character in the film. I have seen poplar trees all my life, from my childhood in Holland, and in Switzerland also. I find them beautiful; they have this shape where all the branches go upwards, they're present near water, their leaves have a particular rustling sound and the bark has a distinct smell. A row of poplar trees lining a canal is a very familiar sight in the Netherlands,[21] recalled the filmmaker. The images of nature (birds, clouds, trees) were integrated not only in order to soften the transitions in the story, but also because "nature has the ability to remind us of timelessness and eternity".[22] The film opens with abstract looking clouds in close-up; then the filmmaker, supported by the main theme from the waltz melody, gradually pulled out:

> When the film starts we have two names in the title, we have two clouds and there is a repetitive theme of two in the whole film (two poplar trees, two sticks coming out of the water). I enjoy playing with subtle repetition, but a spectator shouldn't notice it consciously: otherwise I would have failed.[21]

Claire Jennings, British co-producer of *Father and Daughter*, recalled the labourious genesis of the background's development and

> the many miles I walked to regain a calmness of spirit and perspective on life after Michael having spent many, many months and monies figuring out how the backgrounds on the film could be digitized to reflect his

original vision for the film – rang to let me know he had to start over again using a hand drawn style with charcoal, as the digital styles just weren't working![23]

The filmmaker said that he was delighted to use computers which saved him a lot of time (especially in colouring phase) and contributed to a desired visual impact. As we have seen Dudok de Wit's first drawings were done with 2B and 3B pencils on paper (respectively for the characters and the nature) and charcoal (for the sky, polder and clouds). These drawings were then scanned and converted to a traditional animation software package Animo that also gave to his animation desired colours, textures and contrasted lines. Body and cast shadows were also done in pencil and coloured in Animo, while charcoal backgrounds were scanned and converted into Photoshop for the sake of contrast's adjustments, the cleaning up of drawings and colouring.[24] The images were animated mostly on twos and were later pencil-tested using Take Two software on an Amiga computer.

On the other hand the filmmaker observed that "to give something soul, or to make it really moving in an interesting way, you have to go back to being a hand-drawn animator and just use computers as tools".[25] Hayao Miyazaki would have probably agreed with Dudok de Wit's point of view as he once said: "CGI animators are focused too much on the movement of the characters and very little on their volition. But the movement starts with the volition, and it is this thrust that moves the muscles".[26]

4.4 HEIGHTENED NATURAL AWARENESS OF PENCIL, PAPER AND MOVEMENT

Dudok de Wit met Dutch animator Arjan Wilschut (1971) in London in 1997, during the production of the short film *T.R.A.N.S.I.T.*[27] Just like the letters of the title, the film consisted of seven chapters, and it was animated by different authors. The segment called L'Amerique du Sud Cruiser was animated by Dudok de Wit, while Wilschut worked on the chapter dedicated to the city of Amsterdam. During the production of *T.R.A.N.S.I.T*, Wilschut was very impressed with Dudok de Wit's sequences: "His scene took place at sea and the waves looked amazing, realistic but also very dreamy and hypnotic. Later he told me that waves would often occur in his dreams, which I thought was interesting".[28]

Wilschut himself didn't know personally the filmmaker, but he knew well his film *The Monk and the Fish* much admired for its "philosophical, spiritual and yet playful nature. I must have seen it a hundred times",[28] recalled Wilschut.

Several years later, Dudok de Wit invited Wilschut to London and showed him a storyboard of *Father and Daughter*. They met at his London studio in an old building in the Clerkenwell district. According to the filmmaker, the selection of Wilschut was a good choice from the artistic point of view, and the fact that he was of Dutch origins was not of crucial importance. Dudok de Wit simply recognised that Wilschut's work was "very strong because he did quite realistic human bodies and that was always most challenging for animators".[21] Just watching the storyboard pinned on the wall brought tears to Wilschut's eyes: It was not only because the story moved me, but because it was simply the most beautiful piece of film art I had ever seen! I instantly fell in love with its rhythm, the pacing, the repetition of visual themes and the stylized Dutch landscapes which I remembered from my childhood,[28] recalled Wilschut.

For the next four months the young animator will stay at Dudok de Wit's studio and will share with him "a very special time". The film was made in a pleasant and relaxing working atmosphere: during the working hours, they listened to all kinds of music: from Cesaria Evora to pieces of classical music and even some Dutch pop. They talked about art, movies and played tapes of Eddie Izzard[29] and various audiobooks. They spoke about their homeland and laughed at funny Dutch expressions. Dudok de Wit introduced his young colleague to the work of Hayao Miyazaki and Terrence Malick. Wilschut co-animated with zeal and diligence, but it was not always easy to familiarise with Dudok de Wit's animation style:

> I remember the scene with the old lady walking along-side her bike, against a stiff wind. I remember animating her clothes that were flapping in the wind too smoothly. The pencil test was hilarious, as if she were walking under water. Michael just shook up the drawings in a completely random order and then it worked just fine.[28]

During their collaboration, the young animator observed carefully Dudok de Wit's working method:

> Michael makes his drawings like a Tibetan monk would paint calligraphy. Watching him work taught me another way to animate a drawing: by thinking about the move-ment and visualizing it, and as if you were tracing the line in your mind, you gently put yours on the paper. You put light lines first and get the shape right. Then you make some tiny corrections and re-draw it with just a bit more weight to the line until it's right. It was a sort of height-ened awareness of pencil and paper and movement, a very natural process which I had not experienced before.[28]

Dudok de Wit animated the protagonist with very subtle sensi-bility in which the serenity and stillness prevail. The shape, pos-ture and movements of her body have been changing over time: from brisk and playful movements of a five-year-old to a serene and elegant gait of a middle-aged woman to tired and slow move-ments of an old person.

"I loved drawing that little old lady, although I had to redo a very long scene where her bicycle kept dropping. It was a plea-sure to animate such a nice character with a characteristic look and behavior",[30] said Dudok de Wit.

Light and shadows, the distinguishing characteristics of Dudok de Wit's graphic style, permeate the empty film space. It somehow looks like as if this imaginary Dutch polder became his interior, vibrant heartland, which morphed into the cinematic landscape where "the invisible is only what is too brightly lit".[31] Here again (like in *The Monk and the Fish*) certain scenes seem as if they were lit underneath (especially the opening one) with warm and diffused quality of light. Whenever the protagonist is on the dike, waiting and longing for her father, she looks to the West, always towards the light and the infinite horizon. Then there's a presence of delicate night light, with a full moon and barely recognizable silhouettes of two poplars, shortly altered with the beam of the bicycle's front light. In the final union scene, in a midst of a bare landscape stained only with spare tufts of low grass, the shadows of father and daughter are so neat and the harsh light is so otherworldly. The shadows obviously lack in the scenes where the sun is absent, but instead of them, there is a quiet presence of reflections on the water surface (a small flying bird, sun and horizon reflect themselves in the puddle, avocet bird mirrors itself on the puddle surface). The poetic sensibility of smooth and barely perceptible transitions from one form into another become also a choice in editing.

> I like animating shadows even if this means more work. I would lose all interest in the film if there were no shadows. Without them the drawings become completely flat. And if in the film there is the presence of light, then the graphic beauty of shadows is very strong, especially for tree shadows.[21]

4.5 LONGING IN LONG TAKES

Animation historian Giannalberto Bendazzi qualified *Father and Daughter* as a reassuring classic film.[32] And indeed it contains all distinctive marks of a classic: a prevailing linear narrative and mise-en-scène in its function, configuration of events in a causal order, the main character's quest for a definite purpose, positioning of the main character in the centre of the space, canonical long shots that evolve in subsequent closer shots concentrated around the protagonist, transparent editing that emphasises emotional resonance and continuity between the shots by using ellipsis, eyeline matching and other seamless transitions such as dissolves and morphing, so typical of animation medium.

In *Father and Daughter*, Dudok de Wit could not use any verbal language to help the narrative because he had chosen to make a film without dialogues and the highly emotive and emphatic response grew out from the film's stillness and emptiness which is the result of the richness of film language.

> Like many film makers I tried to use the combined effect of different aspects of film making – like the lighting, the color scheme, the ambience of the landscape and the relationship between the character and the landscape in each scene, the point of view of the camera, the presence of nature, the overall timing and especially the acting, the use of music and of sound – to express emotions.[33]

Dudok de Wit indeed is a classic author, rooted in traditional animation, whose auteur films elaborate archetypal, universal ideas. He was not ashamed to admit that he had recycled[34] ideas from the most admiring works of other classic artists (Hergé, Norstein). And indeed as much as Dudok de Wit's clear line evokes Sempé's and specially Hergé's drawing style, his trait is somehow different in its graphic quality, light and fine or abrasive and trembling at times; his line adapts itself to the expressive force of his inner world. The inspiration that originated from Dumała's murky atmosphere and oblique landscape shadows (*Franz Kafka*) results in even bolder, diagonal charcoal shadows, a sort of cinematic expressionism rarely seen in animation of that period. The timeless atmosphere of the "Eternity" sequence from Yuri Norstein's film *Tale of Tales*, reinforced by Bach's Prelude and Fugue, is reflected in the consistency of suffused light that sculpts the setting at the end of the farewell scene in which the choice of high camera becomes crucial: we see a silhouette of daughter's tiny, agitated body, in backlighting, and her fragility against the majestic sunset. And indeed, in this sublime image, nature is indifferent to her longing, and this becomes even more intense in the winter scene where the whiteness of snow covers everything and the landscape remains intersected only by the feeble outlines of the trees and by the dark traces of polder under the snow. The representations of nature and the change of seasons define the overall atmosphere in *Father and Daughter*. All nature's elements are present in the film: rain, snow, wind, water, clouds. Trees near the canal, thick polder grass, the presence of diverse bird species ("avocet, a goose, a small murmuration of starlings, a skylark when the old lady finds the boat and some birds without any clear identity"[35]) form the topographic map of the landscape. In one scene of haiku sensibility, we see only two fragile branches with the delicate autumn leaves trembling on the strong wind. The foliage is animated with twenty-four drawings per second and coloured in two tonalities of light brown. The feelings of melancholy evolve from the restricted gamut of colours, from "the light source coming almost always from the left, and the perspective opening toward the horizon, to infinity". In fact, this particular quality of harsh, northern light (an antipode to a warm, Mediterranean light of *The Monk and the Fish*), spread over the never-ending Dutch plain fields, enhances the beauty of desolation in woman's yearning. This is overly striking in the family scene in which the woman stands aside on the dike's edge, while her children and husband are close to the water. The sense of longing is imbued in the stillness of this perseverating middle-aged daughter: not just the direction of her gaze but her whole body is gently inclined towards the horizon, towards hope and their final union. In the daughter's serene and abstained motion, the presence of yearning is even more acute: it becomes almost the embodiment of her metaphysical solitude.

4.6   THE SCORE – THE DANUBE WAVES AND BICYCLE BELLS

Dudok de Wit fell in love with the melody of the melancholy waltz called *Waves of the Danube*[36] and decided to embed Ivanović's musical theme[37] in *Father and Daughter* after he had seen Emir Kusturica's feature film *When Father Was Away on*

Business[38] (*Otac na službenom putu*, 1985). When he wrote the storyline for *Father and Daughter*, he immediately contacted Canadian musician Normand Roger,[39] one of the most prolific music composers for short animated films. Collaboration with Roger was a dream come true for Dudok de Wit: they met on the International animation festival in Ottawa in the year the filmmaker presented *The Monk and the Fish*. He particularly loved Roger's score for Frederik Back's film *The Man who Planted Trees:* "I find that music very emotional: especially the gentle tune at the very end of the film when the old shepherd is sitting next to the tree. It is such a beautiful music and such a simple melody".[21]

Roger, shy and friendly in a quiet way,[40] accepted Dudok de Wit's invitation not only because he liked *The Monk and the Fish*, but also because he loved "the art quality and the originality of the screenplay for *Father and Daughter*".[41] The filmmaker showed Roger some variations of the melody and the original recordings from several Eastern European orchestras that he particularly liked, and they agreed to use the old waltz theme because of its "evocation of memories and nostalgia".[42] The filmmaker also explained Roger certain emotions he wanted to imbue in his film. The composer did a recording very early in the project, but Dudok de Wit didn't need it straight away, so they decided to concentrate on the music upon the finished film.

In a long course of his career, Roger developed a particular methodology in the process of composing for an auteur's film. In the first phase, he does a brief interview with a filmmaker in which he asks the author his/her general opinion and intentions about the film and questions about more or less satisfactory parts of the film/screenplay. The successive step is visualisation of a film, and in the end by summing up the interview results, the author's personality and his/her intentions, the composer tries to invent the original musical accompaniment that will be unique exclusively for that specific film.[43] In the case of *Father and Daughter*, the main challenge for Roger was to invent instrumentation variations that would diversify the life chapters of the main character.

"Each chapter starts with a new musical theme with a change in the instrumentation so that the time laps between each chapter could be perceived. The Ivanović's waltz is only used in the beginning and at the end of the film and most of the music is original although written as if it were a musical suite. At the end of the first sequence, when the father goes away in his boat, I introduce a new musical theme that I will use throughout the film whenever the little girl will return to the site of that dramatic departure. Bringing back even a few notes from that theme at the end of those life chapters will suggest to us that the girl is thinking and longing her father",[44] said the composer who successfully rearranged the original orchestral version of the main melody in a yearning variation of accordion solo.

The assignment of sound editing, recording and mixing (sound effects of birds, bicycles, wind, rain, water, leaves, bicycle bells) was left to Roger's son Jean-Baptiste Roger who collaborated with his father on several films in the period from 1998 until 2001. According to Roger, the sound effects of bicycles and tinkling of bicycle bells were of particular relevance for the film since they contributed to the desired effect of nostalgia and the reality of the characters. The symbiosis of the images, clear or smudged, defined by a simple line, thick or sharp, and the music (variations of diverse melodies and musical instruments, the leading melancholy theme of the waltz) invoke the Einfühlung[45] or empathy: the waves of overwhelming emotions of yearning along with sadness and comfort resonate deeply with a spectator.[46] Roger explained how music and visuals woven together create a feeling of empathy: "Once you associate music in a scene in a film, it's not about the music anymore. It's about the impression, and the emotion you create".[47]

Moreover, the score of *Father and Daughter* reinforces the elusive notion of the passing of time. A musical motif associated with the father's departure is present in all ten chapters in different variations. There again the composer intuitively felt that "starting each sequence with a different orchestration from the previous one, which, when combined with the introduction of a new theme, can help suggest the idea that time is passing".[48] In the orchestrations, Roger used six different music instruments.[49] Musician Denis Chartrand, with whom the composer often collaborates, played the piano and the accordion, and two other musicians recorded the bassoon and clarinet arrangements. In all of this, I was looking for simplicity. In each of the musical sequences, I only used two or three instruments, apart from the part with the strings, which are quite discreet anyway. Forcing or driving the emotion in the film could have had a disastrous effect,[50] explained Roger.

An intriguing point of view regarding the use of music in animated shorts is to be found in an irreverent compendium of reflections on the art of animation *The Animation Pimp* written by Chris Robinson[51] who points out that music in films today "doesn't just suggest a tone or a mood, it pinpoints exactly how you should be responding to a scene".[52] Annoyed with the current overuse of film scores and as a fervent fan of "the powers of a silent image", Robinson cleared up:

> *Father and Daughter* is a decent enough film, but when the old broad dies and runs to her father (becoming a young girl again in the process), the music reaches its icky crescendo that destroys the simplicity and authenticity of the rest of the film. Dudok de Wit lost confidence in his ability to simply convey emotions through his images. Conversely, take a look at the films of Igor Kovalyov. Until *Flying Nansen*, he had never used music in any of his films and yet his films convey so much through the movement of the characters, the camera and the editing.[52]

A frustrated musician in his own right, Dudok de Wit observed that his films could be seen as a visual music in a way. "I see in animation the same laws we have in music; I recognize them over and over again. Animation, like music, is about movement and both are time based".[21] Another time he confessed that the music was always like my muse. I knew which music I wanted to have before I started doing storyboards for my shorts. Every time when I had a visual idea, I thought "what would be the perfect music for that?" And in every case the music set the rhythm and the timing of the film in general.[53]

Father and Daughter is a film with no dialogue in which the filmmaker didn't use close-ups and alternated mainly long shots with medium shots. In this specific case, the music becomes the film's necessary ingredient; it gently carries the story on and contributes to better define the mood and appeal to emotions. The apparently simple score with its variations adapted itself to the simplicity of Dudok de Wit's visual language resulting in a powerful synesthesia – wistful visuals and auditory stimuli accompanied a spectator to the heart of the daughter's yearning, relieved in the climax scene of the final reunion.

Dudok de Wit went to Canada to assist in person the final phase of the post-production: The sound mix was finished less than a day before the deadline for the film to be submitted for selection at the Ottawa festival. Michael and I drove two hours from Montreal to Ottawa so that the film could be included five minutes before the deadline! The film was chosen, awarded a prize and the rest is history,[54] concluded Roger.

Father and Daughter was widely acclaimed and won numerous awards throughout the world (BAFTA award, Academy Award for the Best Animated Short Film,[55] awards in Zagreb, Hiroshima, Ottawa, Annecy Grand Prix, Cartoon d'Or), but for Dudok de Wit, one Dutch accolade was especially gratifying: his homeland included *Father and Daughter* on the list of Dutch film classics of all time. The international success of the film has given immense pleasure to the filmmaker: finally it was a clear confirmation that international audiences appreciated it and, on a more personal level, that he had finally found his way.[56]

4.7 CRITICAL RECEPTION OF *FATHER AND DAUGHTER*

Regarding the "acute sensibility" that distinguishes the artworks of Far East (China, Japan), art historian Ernst H. Gombrich observed that Chinese art theorist often analysed the expressive rendering of brush and ink technique by means of absence. In those antique Chinese paintings, there were "things which ten hundred brushstrokes cannot depict but which can be captured by a few simple strokes if they are right. That is truly giving expression to the invisible".[57] This aesthetical idea explains itself in the ancient rule of Chinese painting "I TAO PI PU TAO" which means "if the idea is present, the brush may spare itself the work".[58] Gombrich assumed that a limited graphic language of Chinese art, with its vast empty spaces that are so close to the art of calligraphy, encourages and stimulates observer's integration and elicits his/her interpretative responses. (Empty zones of artwork are filled in by the beholder's imagination.) Similar evocative power of vibrant, empty spaces has been present in Dudok de Wit's art since his youth. But this presence is most evident in *Father and Daughter*, in the film's vast landscapes shot mainly in long takes and with a use of high camera, thus stimulating spectators to project their personal (hi)story in the film.

As for this "painful and yet beautiful absence, that unattainable yearning"[59] in *Father and Daughter*, Dudok de Wit received a great number of moving testimonies from his friends and unknown spectators alike, who told him that the film evoked what they themselves had once experienced. This film functions as the collective mirror of our common vulnerability and resonates with our fragility and ephemerality. The filmmaker pointed out that it was really important to be very sensitive about the viewers' individual interpretations:

> I've had a couple of people coming to me saying that they were touched by the way I treated the theme of death in my film, while other people said this film is not at

all about death. And both are right; each person has an individual view on death which affects the interpretation of the film.[60]

British co-producer Claire Jennings remembers the atmosphere in the edit room at the first viewing of the final mix of *Father and Daughter*:

> I found myself with streams of tears running from my eyes. It was a completely unexpected and startling experience. However when we switched the lights on the sound guys were also quickly turning away whilst wiping their eyes too! Something I'd never witnessed before. This emotional reaction was echoed in the premiere screening we held in London for the industry. A large majority of the room came out after the screening with tears rolling down their faces![61]

The Italian poetess Cettina Caliò Perroni acutely felt that the subtle beauty of *Father and Daughter* "lies in our involvement, in our feelings within the filmmaker's essential and passional pencil trait, in ourselves being those pencil lines. We are pedalling life against the wind. We are life".[62] While animation historian Olivier Cotte observed that watching Dudok de Wit's film is "still a moving experience in which the emotion pours forth from screen and touches you deeply",[63] a film critic Pascal Vimenet saw in it "a veritable visual meditation that represents a vibrating life".[64]

Ed Hooks, actor, writer and acting coach, has been screening Dudok de Wit's film on his workshops dedicated to acting for animators for years and retains *Father and Daughter* one of the strongest, most profound short animations ever created:

> In this film Michael brilliantly had the young girl change over time. She is always pursuing objectives. When she is a little girl, she returns to the spot where her father

died, trying to learn when he would be back, at that point, she did not understand mortality. As she ages, she comes to understand the finality of death and then, because she has a family of her own, she finally connects the dots of life: birth, love, children, death. A perfect cycle, and the bicycle wheel is a metaphor for the circle of life.[65]

Animation historian Giannalberto Bendazzi defined Dudok de Wit's film as

a one-of-a-kind work, like a poem or a painting. It doesn't try to please the audience; it conveys a special feeling and a special appearance, which the audience is free to accept or not. It doesn't mind entertaining or filling some leisure time and it also has a serious message.[66]

Dutch animation director Paul Driessen nominated *Father and Daughter* as a "film close to my heart since it touches our shared Dutch culture".[67] Isao Takahata remembered the moment of a very pleasant shock when he saw *Father and Daughter* for the first time:

I was deeply impressed: this must be the best of the best short animation, I thought. Everything about this work is impressive. I was particularly impressed that while the style is simple, Michael depicted the landscape of the Dutch polder and its structure so precisely and presented it to the audience as a unified world.[68]

This precise, unified world of Dudok de Wit's imaginary Dutch landscape is imbued with melancholy, and this may be another reason why it resonates so well with the spectators. Japanese manga writer and artist Jiro Taniguchi (1947–2017) regarded melancholy as a kind of cure for maintaining one's spiritual balance:

Among human feelings it seems more subtle, elusive and undoubtedly the most precious. Melancholy is considered the purest state of an individual, and therefore also the most vulnerable. I think we should always keep this sort of interstice, of emptiness, in our own spirit, in our own heart.[69]

4.8   THE CONSOLING BEAUTY OF TRANSIENCE

Cycles of life, represented in monochrome visual motifs and expressed with a clear line and the hues of trembling smudges of sepias, browns and pastel blue, the immensity of the evolving Dutch polders, the consoling beauty of the changing of seasons, evoke the tide of exquisite feelings that I find summed up in a Japanese phrase *mono no aware*.[70] This eastern aesthetic ideal "implies the sensibility, the awareness of and responsiveness of something, a refined sensitivity toward the sorrowful and transient nature of beauty, the feeling of being connected to nature and all things".[71] Isao Takahata observed that the film *Father and Daughter* "ends with a scene that moves every kind of audience: a scene that conveys Dudok de Wit's unique – and clearly not Christian – view of life and death that is very close to that of the Japanese".[72] And finally it is in this sophisticated unity of his pencil line and shadowy charcoal landscapes, intertwined with the unadorned storytelling and the delicate timing, that the "eastern quality" of *mono no aware* aura emerges. It is the sum of sensations and sentiments of lyrical qualities we can all experience when contemplating the majesty of nature and the changing of seasons. In our correspondence with Dudok de Wit, I've mentioned once that his films awake *mono no aware* emotional experience in me. He was enthusiastic to discover this exquisitely Japanese ancient way of human interacting with nature, where the issue of transience inevitably appears again:

> The expression *mono no aware* is new to me; I had to look it up. And here too, my reaction is: "of course...!" Of course there is a word for this. The Japanese artists play with this concept in their art and we recognize it. You are right, I have explored this in my films and I feel

it as a compliment when you point that out, because
mono no aware is such a fine and wise way of seeing life.
I love the transience of things.[73]

Dudok de Wit recognised that his being a commercial artist, entertainer and a storyteller is something that remains on surface, whilst
deeper in his creativity, he wanted to express the essence of pain,
beauty, love, nature. He wanted to convey the essence of something
that goes beyond art. Over time, the filmmaker also realised that
his films were actually tools[74] which helped him a lot on his own
spiritual journey. In this sense, the filmmaker's formal research in
the art of animation coincided with the trajectory of his spiritual
quest which resulted in his disclosed ecstatic truth of "a spiritual
longing for the absolute, or for total, unconditional love".[21]

Father and Daughter is again a film about separation and
union, with the daughter's yearning as a main emotion that
reaches its conclusion in the final scene.

> And I think that's life. Human beings live in a state of non-
> separation in very early childhood, but they soon lose it.
> Later they may long for union again when they make love,
> for instance, which is an extraordinary, temporary form
> of union, when they lovingly share adult life with some-
> one or when they travel on the spiritual path. Mystics
> consciously look for union, or they have recognised union
> and after a number of years this recognition becomes fully
> integrated in their everyday lives. The story of this film is
> the story of our lives, and the three phases of this voyage
> consist of an unconscious union to a conscious separation
> until the final, desired conscious union.[2]

In the prevailing long shots of the wistful setting, delineated with
a minimum of graphic means and enlivened by a delicate animation, the intensity of filmmaker's personal feeling is beautifully
transposed in daughter's solitary yearning, exacerbated in spare
autumn and winter landscapes. The daughter's constant, ritual
returns throughout the seasonal repetitions will take us, step by

step, towards her telos – that much desired union and embrace of two shadows that become one in the final scene. Still, there is no sentimentality in Dudok de Wit's unadorned images, graphically distilled into a serene, atemporal visual poetry, which seem to reflect themselves in the following verses of a wandering Swiss poet Robert Walser[75]:

> I only know that it's quiet here,
> stripped of all needs and doings,
> here it feels good, here I can rest
> for no time measures my time.[76]

NOTES

1. Kurosawa, Akira, *Something Like an Autobiography*, Vintage Books, New York, 1983, p. 105.
2. Michael Dudok de Wit to Andrijana Ružić, London, 7 December 2018.
3. Polder is a tract of low land reclaimed from a body of water (such as the sea). The Merriam-Webster.com Dictionary, Merriam-Webster Inc., https://www.merriam-webster.com/dictionary/polder, retrieved 21 January 2020.
4. Dudok de Wit, Michael, *Vader en Dochter*, Leopold, Amsterdam, 2015, p. 23.
5. I'm grateful to the film producer Willem Thijssen who noted one important aspect that needed ulterior explanation: "The fact that the water on which the father rows away in the beginning has disappeared! So the old lady can go by foot to the leftovers of the boat in the end. She walks through the high grass of the new polder towards the wracked boat. The fact that the Dutch take the water away to create more land, is shown here very clearly and this is an important item for a small country like Holland. During the preproduction this was the background of my (not accepted) title proposition 'waterloos'". Willem Thijssen's email to Andrijana Ružić, 19 March 2020.
6. Piotr Dumała (1956) is a Polish director and animator, illustrator and writer. He graduated at the Warsaw Academy of fine arts in sculpture conservation and later in animation. Dumała is known for his specific ephemeral animation technique consisting in scratching images into painted plaster, subsequently erased and

repainted one image after another, frame after frame. His memorable monochrome and oneiric short films, to mention only a few, *Franz Kafka* (1991) and *Crime and Punishment* (2000), won numerous accolades all around the world. Dumała teaches animation in Europe and USA.

7. Kawa-Topor, Xavier, Nguyên, Ilan, *Michael Dudok de Wit. Le cinéma d'animation sensible. Entretien avec le réalisa-teur de La Tortue Rouge*, Capricci, Paris, 2019, p. 52.

8. Willem Thijssen email to Andrijana Ružić, 21 August 2017.

9. Michael Dudok de Wit to Andrijana Ružić, Interview on Mirogoj cemetery, Zagreb, Croatia, 9 June 2017.

10. The story of *Father and Daughter* is not based on Dudok de Wit's personal experience; his both parents were alive at the time.

11. Cotte, Olivier, *Secrets of Oscar-Winning Animation*, Focal Press, New York and London, 2006, p. 229.

12. The only exceptions are the protagonist's companion and her little son that appear in two scenes.

13. Kawa-Topor, Xavier, Nguyên, Ilan, *Michael Dudok de Wit. Le cinéma d'animation sensible. Entretien avec le réalisa-teur de La Tortue Rouge*, Capricci, Paris, 2019, p. 64.

14. Kawa-Topor, Xavier, Nguyên, Ilan, *Michael Dudok de Wit. Le cinéma d'animation sensible. Entretien avec le réalisa-teur de La Tortue Rouge*, Capricci, Paris, 2019, p. 53.

15. Michael Dudok de Wit to Andrijana Ružić, London, 8 December 2018.

16. Wells, Paul, Quin, Joanna, Mills, Les, *Basics Animation 03: Drawing for Animation*, An AVA Book, Lausanne, 2009, pp. 162–165.

17. Willem Thijssen email to Andrijana Ružić, 21 August 2017.

18. Furniss, Maureen, *The Animation Bible*, Abrams, New York, 2008, p. 200.

19. Kawa-Topor, Xavier, Nguyên, Ilan, *Michael Dudok de Wit. Le cinéma d'animation sensible. Entretien avec le réalisa-teur de La Tortue Rouge*, Capricci, Paris, 2019, p. 61.

20. Furniss, Maureen, *The Animation Bible*, Abrams, New York, 2008, p. 201.

21. Michael Dudok de Wit to Andrijana Ružić, London, 6 December 2018.

22. Wells, Paul, Quin, Joanna, Mills, Les, *Basics Animation 03: Drawing for Animation*, An AVA Book, Lausanne, 2009, pp. 162–165.

23. Claire Jennings email to Andrijana Ružić, 1 May 2019.
24. Cotte, Olivier, *Secrets of Oscar-Winning Animation*, Focal Press, New York and London, 2006, p. 239.
25. Hourigan, Jonathan, *A Conversation with Michael Dudok de Wit*, http://www.robert-bresson.com/Words/Dudok_de_Wit.html, retrieved 9 October 2019.
26. Arakawa, Kaku, documentary film *Never-Ending Man– Hayao Miyazaki*, NHK, 2017.
27. *T.R.A.N.S.I.T* was written and directed by Dutch animation director Piet Kroon (1960).
28. Arjan Wilschut's email to Andrijana Ružić, 28 September 2017.
29. Eddie Lizzard (1962) is an English stand-up comic, actor and writer.
30. Hourigan, Jonathan, *A Conversation with Michael Dudok de Wit*, http://www.robert-bresson.com/Words/Dudok_de_Wit.html, retrieved 9 October 2019.
31. Lerner, Ben, *A Strange Australian Masterpiece*, The New Yorker, 29 March 2017, https://www.newyorker.com/books/page-turner/a-strange-australian-masterpiece, retrieved 5 January 2020.
32. Bendazzi, Giannalberto, *Animation: A World History: Volume III*, CRC Press, New York, 2016, p. 115.
33. Wells, Paul, Quin, Joanna, Mills, Les, *Basics Animation 03: Drawing for Animation*, An AVA Book, Lausanne, 2009, pp. 162–165.
34. Kawa-Topor, Xavier, Nguyên, Ilan, *Michael Dudok de Wit. Le cinéma d'animation sensible. Entretien avec le réalisa-teur de La Tortue Rouge*, Capricci, Paris, 2019, p. 183.
35. Michael Dudok de Wit's email to Andrijana Ružić, 14 March 2020.
36. Influenced by the music of Johann Strauss, the waltz was composed in 1880 by the Romanian composer of Serbian origin, Jovan Ivanović (1845–1902).
37. Dudok de Wit heard this melody for the first time in the seventies, in Jim Capaldi's rock version of it called *Anniversary Song (Oh How We Danced)*.
38. It is interesting to note that the film plot of Kusturica's feature is also based on father's absence, while the story is narrated in the first person by the youngest child in the family, Malik. A film-maker Emir Kusturica (Sarajevo 1954), with the talents of an actor and a musician, is one of the most internationally acclaimed film directors from the ex-Yugoslav cultural area.

39. A self-taught musician Normand Roger (1949) has been working as a free-lance composer and sound designer for National Film Board of Canada since 1972. In his forty-year long career, he has been credited for more than 200 scores for short animated films. He has done music for six short films that won an Academy award, out of 13 nominated. Roger also composes for documentaries, feature films, TV commercials and does music installations for museums and fairs.

40. Michael Dudok de Wit to Andrijana Ružić, Interview on Mirogoj cemetery, Zagreb, Croatia, 9 June 2017.

41. Cotte, Olivier, *Secrets of OscarWinning Animation*, Focal Press, New York and London, 2006, p. 245.

42. Normand Roger's email to Andrijana Ružić, 3 August 2017.

43. Martignoni, Andrea, *Ascolto cinetico. I concetti musicali di Normand Roger*, in Bendazzi, Cecconello, Michelone, *Coloriture. Voci, rumori, musiche nel cinema d'animazione*, Pendragon, Bologna, 1995, p. 180.

44. Normand Roger email to Andrijana Ružić, 9 August 2017.

45. German word Einfühlung ("feeling into") appears for the first time in 1873, in German philosopher Robert Vischer's doctoral dissertation on Aesthetics. With the term "Einfühlung", Vischer intended to explain the human capacity to enter into a work of art (figurative art, literature, music) and feel the emotions that the artist aimed to represent in it. The English term for "Einfühlung" is empathy – the ability to share an emotion viscerally.

46. For its emphatic resonance with a spectator, *Father and Daughter* has been used as a case study in pedagogical and psychological studies. In the book *The Professional Development of Teachers Educators*, edited by Tony Bates, Anja Swennen, Ken Jones, Routledge, 2014, p. 161/162, the film was used as "a metaphor for development" within the context of a narrative dialogical concept of professional identity. *Father and Daughter* has also been discussed by Monika Suckfuell in her interdisciplinary study *Films That Move Us: Moments of Narrative Impact in an Animated Short Film*. https://www.berghahn-journals.com/view/journals/projections/4/2/proj040204.xml retrieved 10 July 2018.

47. Hofferman, Jon, *Sound of Animation: An Interview with Normand Roger*, World Network, 2008, https://www.awn.com/animationworld/sound-animation-interview-normand-roger, retrieved 25 July 2018.

48. Cotte, Olivier, *Secrets of Oscar-Winning Animation*, Focal Press, New York and London, 2006, p. 246.
49. Roger used accordion, piano, bassoon, guitar, clarinet and strings.
50. Cotte, Olivier, *Secrets of Oscar-Winning Animation*, Focal Press, New York and London, 2006, p. 246.
51. Chris Robinson (1967) is arguably the most unorthodox writer about animation so far and artistic director of the Ottawa International Animation Festival.
52. Robinson, Chris, *The Animation Pimp*, AWN Press, Los Angeles, 2007, p. 123.
53. Barlow, Dominic, *The Red Turtle*, Interview with Michael Dudok de Wit, 4:3, 20 September 2016 https://fourthreefilm. com/2016/09/the-red-turtle-an-interview-with-michael-dudok-de-wit/ retrieved 4 September 2018.
54. Cotte, Olivier, *Secrets of Oscar-Winning Animation*, Focal Press, New York and London, 2006, p. 247.
55. Dudok de Wit remains in the archives of the 73rd Academy Awards as a filmmaker who gave the shortest acceptance speech in Los Angeles, on 25 March 2001. This fact had impressed also an animation historian Charles Solomon who even calculated the duration of the speech – eighteen seconds. When Dudok de Wit received an Oscar statuette from the host-actor Ben Stiller, he had addressed the invited guests with the following words:
    I would like to thank my two producers, Claire Jennings from London and Willem Thijssen from Amsterdam, both for their dedication and very hard work. And I would like to thank especially my wife Arielle for her support. Thank you, Academy members, this is fantastic. http://aaspeechesdb.oscars.org/link/073-17/, retrieved on 1 May 2018.
56. Kawa-Topor, Xavier, Nguyên, Ilan, *Michael Dudok de Wit. Le cinéma d'animation sensible. Entretien avec le réalisa-teur de La Tortue Rouge*, Capricci, Paris, 2019, p. 65.
57. Gombrich, Ernst H., *Art and Illusion. A Study in the Phycology of Pictorial Representation*, Pantheon Books, New York, 1960, p. 209.
58. Munari, Bruno, *Arte come mestiere*, Gius. Laterza & Figli, Bari, 2018, p. 228. translated from Italian by Andrijana Ružić.
59. *Interview with Michael Dudok de Wit*, Press Kit Wild Bunch Interviews with artists, Wild Bunch International Sales, https://www.wildbunch.biz/movie/the-red-turtle/, last retrieved 2 February 2018.

60. Vimeo interview with Michael Dudok de Wit, https://vimeo.com/29664893, retrieved 1 March 2018.
61. Claire Jennings email to Andrijana Ružić, 1 May 2019.
62. Cettina Caliò Perroni's email to Andrijana Ružić, 7 October 2019.
63. Cotte, Olivier, *Secrets of Oscar-Winning Animation*, Focal Press, New York and London, 2006, p. 247.
64. Merlin, Geneviève, *Michael Dudok de Wit. La Tortue Rouge*, Atlande, Neuilly, 2018, p. 26.
65. Ed Hooks's email to Andrijana Ružić, 25 June 2019.
66. Bendazzi, Giannalberto, *Animation: A World History: Volume III*, CRC Press, New York, 2016, p. 115.
67. Paul Driessen email to Andrijana Ružić, 14 July 2018.
68. *Interview with Isao Takahata*, Press Kit, Wild Bunch International Sales, https://www.wildbunch.biz/movie/the-red-turtle/, last retrieved 2 February 2018.
69. *L'autore di manga con lo sguardo da bambino*, Intervista a Jiro Taniguchi, in *Taniguchi, Jiro, La mono no aware*, Rizzoli-Lizard, Milano 2019, p. 200. Translated from Italian by Andrijana Ružić.
70. The connotations of the phrase *mono no aware* diverge around interpretations of *aware*. Use of the Chinese character for 'sad' to render Japanese word aware associates *mono no aware* with sad or fleeting experiences. That nuance is not, however, intrinsic to the phrase, whose essence is the experience of being deeply moved by emotions that may include joy, love and sadness as well. It is Motoori Norinaga (1730–1801) to whom we owe our understanding of *mono no aware*. In his writings, examining the concept, Norinaga noted that experiencing *mono no aware* means savouring life more deeply. Exhibition Overview. "Mono no Aware" and Japanese beauty, April 17–June 16, 2013, Suntory Museum of Art, Tokyo, Japan, https://www.suntory.com/sma/exhibition/2013_2/display.html retrieved on 10 October 2018.
71. Shimoda, Todd, *"Oh" a Mystery of "mono no aware"*, https://ohthenovel.wordpress.com/mononoaware/, last retrieved 21 October 2018.
72. *Interview with Isao Takahata*, Press Kit, Wild Bunch International Sales, https://www.wildbunch.biz/movie/the-red-turtle/, last retrieved 2 February 2018.
73. Michael Dudok de Wit's email to Andrijana Ružić, 20 October 2018.

74. Kawa-Topor, Xavier, Nguyên, Ilan, *Michael Dudok de Wit. Le cinéma d'animation sensible. Entretien avec le réalisa-teur de La Tortue Rouge*, Capricci, Paris, 2019, p. 147.
75. Born in Biel, Switzerland, Robert Walser (1878–1956) was a German speaking poet and novelist. He published his work in his home country only after 1920. Inclined to solitary life, he spent his last years in a psychiatric hospital in Herisau. Misunderstood by critics for a long period, he gained worldwide appreciation only after his death.
76. *Oppressive Light*. Selected poems by Robert Walser, translated and edited by Daniele Pantano, Black Lawrence Press Schaeferstunde/ Tryst, p. 20.

CHAPTER 5

The Aroma of Tea (2006) – A Blissful Experience

Form is empty and emptiness is form.

THE HEART SUTRA

THE TRIUMPHANT SUCCESS OF *Father and Daughter* bolstered Dudok de Wit's desire to make his most essential, monochromatic and non-figurative short film *The Aroma of Tea*. "It was the right moment for Michael to make an old 'dream' come true, to do a new short film, less 'commercial' and almost experimental",[1] said Willem Thijssen, the Dutch film producer.[2]

The idea for this fluid film was already alive and simmering somewhere in me. One day in Kassel, Germany, where I was teaching, I was walking on the street, thinking about the music for this particular visual style I had in mind and, suddenly, I remembered that piece by Corelli that I had heard on the radio several years earlier,[3] recalled Dudok de Wit.

On his return to London, he immediately started to develop a story which is, again, as was the case with his previous films, very simple. The provisional title of the film was *Voyage*: the journey of a small dark-brown pulsating dot tirelessly making its way through brownish meanders and void spaces. Between these visually striking organic shapes of soaked tea texture, with microfibers still present in the liquid, the little dot is clearly on a mission. There is a pure yearning, yet again, on this trip. The dot is on a quest for something; it meets others; it persistently searches, and, in the end, it finally reaches home.

The original artwork was intended to be done in black ink, because of the shapes and forms, but he wanted something different, a new technique that had probably never been used before in animation. His initial idea was to paint with blood, but he wasn't satisfied with the brown nuances of the obtained result. The next attempt was with Clipper organic tea that he boiled down in order to concentrate the liquid. The procedure was followed by a further experiment: he exposed, for a couple of weeks, three blobs of tea on a cardboard to direct sunlight, on his studio windowsill. The trial was a success: the dark brown colour also turned out to be very stable. The filmmaker explained:

> My idea was to experiment with highly concentrated tea that becomes a very dark brown liquid, like thick ink. It was also related to the title because there is something about tea that is very pure and simple, and very complex at the same time, and it comes from the East. I thought that suited the film. The title alludes to the ink, which is tea, but it also alludes to the finesse of tea itself, and the finesse of smelling.[4]

In the space of two months, he painted the entire film by himself in his London studio. A Dutch animator/editor, Marc Schopman, operating from his studio in Antwerp in Belgium, was responsible for the compositing, and Nic Gill oversaw the sound editing. Dudok de Wit emailed each finished background to Schopman,

together with a drawn guide indicating the exact path and movement of the dot. Schopman sent back the results, and Dudok de
Wit adjusted them occasionally. The entire film slowly emerged
from this two-way exchange between London and Antwerp.

> Everything evolved so smoothly. I was alone and the
> work was both exciting and meditative. The animation
> process was also simple: I didn't have to worry about
> complex character animation. Many of the typical tech-
> nical challenges were absent, and because the produc-
> tion was progressing at the speed that I had planned, the
> deadline stress was minimal.[3]

Having been inspired by Arcangelo Corelli's *Concerti grossi* opus
6 also meant that he had to use the right orchestra for his film.
After a brief search, Dudok de Wit selected an interpretation of
Corelli's piece by Harmonia Mundi's Swiss orchestra, Ensemble
415, whose repertoire of Italian baroque music stood out by its
rigorous technical approach and use of authentic musical instruments from the baroque period. The fact that he was drawing from Corelli's music again was secondary in a way. "There
is something in the emotion and the choice of instruments in
Corelli. When I first heard that composition, I stopped moving,
I probably stopped breathing. I was hypnotised by its beauty",[5]
commented the filmmaker who generally uses only a limited
number of instruments and small orchestras for his short films.
Corelli's *Concerti grossi* opus 6, with its solemn rhythm, repetitions and gravitas guided the hand of Dudok de Wit the painter:

> I felt that the combination of Concerto 12 with *The
> Aroma of Tea* visuals would be ideal. However, the begin-
> ning of Concerto 12 was not quite right for the start of
> the film. It has a pleasant opening, but it is not striking,
> while the film needed to start with a stronger statement.
> It became quickly obvious that I should start the film
> with another piece, and I chose a 50-second section of

another Concerto Grosso, Concerto 2, a beautiful, slow section with a feeling of anticipation. Since both compositions were in F major, editor Nic Gill simply edited them together into one seamless whole.[6]

The filmmaker consequently mapped out the music and timed the entire film on the score, in a meticulous procedure echoing the one used for *The Monk and the Fish*. He repeatedly listened to the music, day after day, for the sake of the structure:

> Creating a synchronization between music and visuals is like creating a dance. The film was about serenity and infinity and I noticed with awe how this was resonating with a deep part of myself. Besides, since I was working mostly alone, the work was also physically very personal. I stayed for long periods in a zone.[3]

The power of *The Aroma of Tea* lies in its graphic simplicity and in the perfect synergy between its score and visuals. Actually, it looks like as if the filmmaker has surrendered completely to Corelli's composition and thus achieved to transpose its majestic rhythm into a visual metaphor of life. This film can be considered as director's personal homage to the beauty and elegance of Japanese calligraphy which he first discovered in the early eighties at the London Royal Academy of Arts' *The Great Japan Exhibition* dedicated to the artists of the Edo period (1600–1868).

Dudok de Wit's fascination with the culture of Zen Buddhism and Japanese art in general was already apparent in the calligraphic quality of the brush stroke and the storyline of *The Monk and the Fish*. The simplicity of his graphic style echoed that of the Japanese and oriental view of nature: life and death are at the core of *Father and Daughter*. Now, in *The Aroma of Tea*, the grace of these calligraphic visuals hint at the tea ceremony and the principles of Zen Buddhism. The filmmaker observed that

> there is a coherence between almost all of my films. They have a presence of water, of fluidity, and they were inspired

by art from Japanese and Chinese calligraphers, in other words by shapes created with liquid ink. I usually don't even know what their calligraphic characters mean; I'm simply driven by the fluid beauty of calligraphy itself.[3]

The Aroma of Tea was selected on thirty-five international film festivals but was never rewarded by any prize. The initial reception was generally indifferent, and Dudok de Wit was disappointed.[7]

> Some people have seen too much in this film, I think, judging by some comments I have received, and maybe the title is sometimes misleading. I would like the audience to see the film as my symbolic interpretation of union, where the dot dissolves into where it belongs. In my previous short films, I have explored the same universal theme. You don't need to be on a spiritual path to sense this union. In the ending of the film, I just hope that some spectators intuitively recognize that there is something more than a dot dissolving graciously into a circular shape.[3]

According to Dudok de Wit, following the release of *The Aroma of Tea*, even Japanese director Isao Takahata was preoccupied that he might persist with short abstract films and suggested a return to narrative films. However, New York City based animator, director and producer Michael Sporn (1946–2014) appreciated very much the short. Commenting on his blog about the animation category in the Academy awards 2006, he declared:

> Michael Dudok de Wit's *The Aroma of Tea* is a quite beautiful and delicate film. I'm not sure how this abstraction will go over with Academy voters, but I found it excellent. As a matter of fact, there were a couple of wholly abstract films, and I was pleased to see this. Not all of them were as successful as Michael Dudok de Wit's work, but he is undoubtedly a master.[8]

The background of *The Aroma of Tea*, formed by intertwined, fluid, hazel shapes and large sections of empty surfaces that define each other, stands for the inner landscape, a personal geography of the searching dot jolting towards infinity. At the end, it dissolves in a closed, white circle delineated by a spread of tea brown paint. And this white circle, reminiscent of the ancient ensō symbol,[9] could indeed stand for a metaphor of infinity, the final home, the absolute.

I realized in my twenties that my path as a creative person and my path as a seeker were the same. I became aware that my deepest, intuitive longing was for something extraordinary that is neither visible, nor audible. I sometimes call that the absolute. Though it's not a perfect word, it's one of the best I can think of. When you fully realize the absolute, you are conscious of simplicity and of freedom and you feel deeply fulfilled ... you are at home, you have arrived where you belong. At the same time, that home is what you are. And that is what everybody wants: to be home. Home is not affected by the senses, but you can be conscious of it through the senses: with a piece of music, a film, a dance, the simple joy of floating in water. Ultimately, nothing can really describe it. Not a religious text, not the words of a mystic and not even a symbol, because of its incredible, absolute nature. Even words like love or God are inadequate,[3] said Dudok de Wit.

If there is truth in the idea that a brush line reveals the calligrapher's state of mind at the precise moment in time it is drawn, then Dudok de Wit's creative moment was one clearly arising from a sense of serenity and accomplishment as he finally found the right shape for his content. *The Aroma of Tea* is Dudok de Wit's most personal film and, I dare say, even a sort of autobiographical narrative, representing a spontaneous graphical preamble for his first feature film *The Red Turtle*, the sum of his artistic achievements, conceptually based on a single image – that of an earth brown thick arched line painted with a brush.

NOTES

1. Michael Dudok de Wit's email to Andrijana Ružić, 9 September 2017.
2. *The Aroma of Tea* was produced by Thijssen's production studio CinéTé, the Dutch Filmfund and with the support of ARTE France.
3. Michael Dudok de Wit to Andrijana Ružić, London, 7 December 2018.
4. Mitchell, Ben, *The Films of Michael Dudok de Wit – Interview and Competition*, Skwigly Online Animation Magazine, 31 July 2018, http://www.skwigly.co.uk/michael-dudok-de-wit/ retrieved 21 September 2018.
5. Michael Dudok de Wit's email to Andrijana Ružić, 22 March 2020.
6. Michael Dudok de Wit's mail to Andrijana Ružić, 23 March 2020.
7. The producer Willem Thijssen was much more positive about the film's reception: In Japan (including Ghibli), Australia and France the film was acquired for distribution/DVD/TV. Screenings were held in Poland, Canada, Russia, The Netherlands, USA, Spain, United Kingdom, Italy, Slovakia, Hungary, Georgia, Belgium and on Shorts TV in USA & Europe. Another aspect of the film was the distribution in The Netherlands, Dudok de Wit's home country. Since the film was only 3 minutes long it seemed ideal for distribution as a short accompanying a feature at the cinemas. But after a long search not one distributor was willing to do it (and buy the number of prints necessary for such a release in these old (analogical) cinema days. Some years later, Thijssen was appointed the first "animation intendant" with the Dutch Film Fund, and there he introduced the format "Ultra Short". Starting from 2010, the Fund would support on annual basis four short animated films (maximum 2 min) to be made after a contest for story-boards between Dutch animators and a producer. Subsequently the agreement was made directly between the Fund and a big Dutch cinema chain to screen 4 films each year as a short before selected "blockbusters" in order to reach a large audience for them. "And that's what happened and is still going on today in 2020! It was of great help for the development of the Dutch animation sector. All this thanks to *The Aroma of Tea*!" Willem Thijssen's email to Andrijana Ružić, 20 March 2020.

8. Sporn, Michael, *Animated Oscars*, 13 November 2006, http://www.michaelspornanimation.com/splog/?p=847, retrieved 3 November 2018.
9. Enso̅, a circle of the Zen Buddhism, represents the beginning and the end of all things, the circle of life, the universe, infinity, enlightenment.

CHAPTER 6

Coronation of a Dream

The Making of The Red Turtle –
*Michael Dudok de Wit's Ten-
Year-Long "Exciting Challenge",
set by Studio Ghibli and
Completed in Europe*

...so that the image might be experienced first as an emotion...[1]

YURI NORSTEIN

Dudok de Wit said that the most bizarre experience in his career happened on 22 November 2006 when he received a rather unusual email from the Tokyo-based, world-renowned animation Studio Ghibli which literally read:

> Both Isao Takahata and Hayao Miyazaki are very much impressed with *Father and Daughter* and its very unique and beautiful style. We would like to propose that you create an animated feature with us.[2]

Studio Ghibli had never made a film outside of Japan before and their offer to co-produce Dudok de Wit's first feature sounded quite unbelievable. What was even more incredible was their apparent willingness to embrace a distinctive, personal style, different from that usually found in Japanese animated features. The directors of Studio Ghibli always maintained absolute creative control over their films, and this uncompromising auteur's approach to filmmaking was equally central to Dudok de Wit's work ethic. Their future collaboration would be based on mutual admiration and shared affinities, although the cultural and language gap certainly enriched both parties.[3] Animation director Isao Takahata (1935–2018), co-founder of Studio Ghibli, credited as artistic producer in *The Red Turtle*, would give advice and provide feedback but would never interfere with Dudok de Wit's decisions. Amazed and honoured in equal measure, the filmmaker accepted the risk. "I thought that it would be a challenge, but a very exciting challenge".[4] It was the chance of a lifetime and the beginning of an unfolding list of challenges that would crop up one after another, year after year.

6.1 THE PLOT

During a wild tempest in the dark of night, fighting for his life between gigantic waves, a man is cast ashore on a small tropical island populated by a small number of animals. A long strip of bamboo forest skirting the lagoon is the only shelter he can rely on. The castaway's only desire is to flee the place as soon as possible; the deserted island certainly doesn't feel like home. He starts by building a bamboo raft, but as soon as he manages to pass through the coral reef, a mysterious, invisible sea creature shreds it to pieces. On the third attempt, the castaway finds himself face to face with a giant red turtle, gazing at him, before shattering the raft once more. Later that same afternoon, the marine creature appears on the beach, spurring the man's vindictive fury. He turns it over on its back, leaves it there to die and goes to sleep. The restless man's dream about the dead oceanic creature levitating towards the sky introduces a new character to the story. Upon awakening, the incredulous protagonist finds a young red-haired woman sleeping inside the turtle's empty carapace. She eventually wakes up, chastely accepting his worn-out shirt to cover herself. She offers him her hand and her forgiveness in the colourless silence of the warm evening.

Man and woman gradually become a couple, and the island finally turns into their home. The arrival of their son is a new experience for both: they teach him about life and where he comes from. Together they share the moments of adversity and blissfulness hurled at and bestowed on them by nature. With the departure of their grown-up son, who sets for the horizon escorted by his fellow turtles, a new phase in their life begins: old age. Their tranquil life unfolds in harmony with nature, as their hair turns grey and their movements steadily slow down. The narrative line follows the contours of a full life cycle, reaching its final stage in a serene, poignant scene in which the man peacefully dies beside the woman. Transforming herself into a red turtle once again, she slowly disappears towards the horizon, returning to her pelagic origins.

6.2 THE STORYTELLING

> The story is not just a mere event; it is primarily an expression of a particular life principle.[5]
>
> ANTE ZANINOVIĆ

Every challenge in animation starts with a story, and Dudok de Wit needed to find a very good one as soon as possible.

"I wouldn't consider making a film unless the story was worth telling. I also want it to be commercial enough and not just disappear into obscurity after two months at a few festivals",[6] he explained.

Ever since childhood, the filmmaker was fascinated by myths and fables. Ten years previously, he had written and illustrated two books dedicated to children that treated, in a simple way, the problematic issues such as the fear of the dark, understanding death and the cycles of growth in nature.[7] The idea for the feature story came up spontaneously, and he knew from the outset that the film would not revolve around a tale of survival in a classic, Robinson Crusoe-like manner. Instead it was to be a fable about a castaway on an uninhabited island, recounted from a fresh perspective and with a new sensitivity.[8] A remarkable mixture of various inspirational sources moulded Dudok de Wit's fable: tales from the classical Greek mythology, the Robinson Crusoe TV series from the sixties, Hearn's *Kwaidan* book,[9] the principles of the Zen Buddhist philosophy ("It appeals to me and resonates with me deeply"[10]), Taoist philosophy and its relationship with nature and the archetypal idea of infinity associated with the figure of the marine turtle.

"For me, the turtle symbolizes being at ease with infinity", the filmmaker explained. "It doesn't stay near the coast, it goes away for thousands of miles, alone, peacefully, and may not come back for a year or two. She belongs there and leaves the ocean only when she absolutely has to".[11]

The themes he wanted to develop further in his feature (some of them already present in his previous films) are the strong bonds that tie man to nature, struggles with the adversities of life and the transience of life. But he also felt he needed to add something more:

> I deeply respect the unconscious, not just how it feeds our dreams and our imagination, but also how it influences our everyday lives. The more I look at that, the

more I see everyday life not only as a solid and complex reality, where things are divided between subjective and objective, for instance, but also, on a finer level, as fluid, vibrant life, which is all-inclusive and unaffected by any divisions. So, I came from that two-level perspective when I wrote the story.[2]

A hybrid form between myth and fable was a perfect framework to string together all these ideas; only the magical realism of a fable and a myth, structured as a quest for purpose in the world, could properly illustrate the essence of his concepts.

Dudok de Wit immediately started working on the script, which took him several months. At the beginning, the script contained dialogues as he retained them necessary to describe the characters' motivations and to create more empathy towards them. When the script was finished, he started storyboarding and creating the animatic at the same time. At times this process progressed well, but it took a longer time than expected because some sequences didn't flow. There were some distinct knots in the story that the filmmaker couldn't resolve.[2] The solution was to go back to the script and rewrite the whole sections. The decision to involve the French director and scriptwriter Pascale Ferran[12] as a co-writer turned out to be a fortunate choice. Dudok de Wit and Ferran continued to develop the script over the next couple of months.

We had in-depth discussions about the film as we were unable to change discrete elements without affecting the overall balance. She helped me identify problems and make the narrative clearer and more powerful. She also loved the idea that, in animation films, the editing is so well thought out before proceeding with the scenes. She made very valuable contributions to this process,[13] explained Dudok de Wit.

Pascale Ferran was particularly inspired by the filmmaker's beautiful black and white drawings in the animatic.

> I instantly developed a sense of intimacy with the film, probably because it is close to my relationship to the world: the intertwining of life and death, the prevalence of nature, the enchantment of fables. But also, perhaps, because of its most Japanese aspect: our relationship to adversity. At given times, catastrophes occur and we must accept them, we must face them and then rebuild.[14]

For Ferran, the task was simple; the parts of the story that needed to be strengthened were the ones relating to the characters of the woman and the child. She reckoned it was vital to develop the idea of heritage. Heritage not only in reference to the scene of the parents drawing the story of a family in the sand, but also on a "cosmogonic level", pointing out the fact that "nature, from which we all come, is a sort of shared heritage, transmitting things that we will, in turn, have to pass on".

Dudok de Wit believes that the endings are the most powerful moments in short films, and for both *The Monk and the Fish* and *Father and Daughter*, he knew from the beginning how their final scenes will look like. But with *The Red Turtle*, it was different, and during one inspiring walk through the capital of France, he decided to change its ending.

> The first version of the film's ending was the son's departure – he says goodbye to his parents and swims towards the horizon in the company of three turtles. It was a quiet ending with some of this fine sadness to it: the son leaves and succeeds where his father had not succeeded – for me that was a completion. But then one day, while I was walking along the streets of Paris to buy some drawing paper, I came across Montparnasse, a large and beautiful cemetery with tall trees. I thought: how about continuing the story and in the end, we see the father die? But then, what happens to the mother? The idea of the end of the man's life moved me; I literally had tears in my

eyes. It would be a serene death. I immediately contacted Pascale Ferran and told her that I had a new ending.[15]

With the new film's ending, Ferran then suggested fleshing out the details of the couple's life, particularly after the son's departure, in order to reinforce the notion that "we are only passing through this world".[14]

Another important contributor to the script's development was French editor Céline Kélépikis. She had previously collaborated with the producers of Prima Linea Productions who suggested she helps the filmmaker find the right narrative voice. Kélépikis said that the biggest challenge was to hit that fine-tuned balance and rhythm that would capture the spectators' attention. The most difficult part, Kélépikis reckons, was inventing the son's childhood and striking the right balance between sounds and music. One of the best decisions she and Dudok de Wit ever made was to not reveal where the turtle came from and thus preserve an aura of mystery.

Finally, I'm very happy that the long version of Michael's way of telling emotional stories works. When I saw his short films, I was reminded of the simplicity of communicating emotions without words ... the final challenge was to make it work in a feature film,[16] concluded the enthusiastic editor.

At a certain point, Studio Ghibli's producer Toshio Suzuki suggested abandoning the idea of dialogue all together in order to tighten up the film further yet. Dudok de Wit accepted his advice with relief, convinced that the film's visual language and the characters' strong body language should be expressive enough. When new collaborators would arrive to become part of the production team, he would ask them to watch the complete animatic, including the soundtrack. Afterwards they would tell him how they had not really noticed the absence of dialogue or that the absence felt natural. This confirmed to him that he was on the right track and that the film was speaking without any verbal language.

6.3 A UNIQUE COLLABORATIVE EFFORT ON THE VISUAL DEVELOPMENT OF *THE RED TURTLE*

Michael always used to say, "our film" or "the film", I have never heard him say "my film".[17]

JULIEN DE MAN, BACKGROUND SUPERVISOR

In the summer of 2007, the script was approved by Isao Takahata and Toshio Suzuki, the producers of Studio Ghibli. They said they would co-produce the film with Wild Bunch, their distributor in France, and that it would be made in France with European artists only.

Upon final approval of the script and the accompanying drawings, Dudok de Wit proceeded with a storyboard and animatic, and this extremely creative phase took him four years. Although the filmmaker occasionally had the support of collaborators, he mostly worked alone and enjoyed the assistance of occasional collaborators[18]; he mostly completed it by himself. The main reason he required isolation was the need to experiment. ("I needed to make lots of mistakes and learn from them".[19])

When the animatic was finished and producers announced a budget, a team was put together: character animators, special effects animators, background artists, editors, and other professionals. The number of people involved in the project at any one time would vary between twenty-five and forty-five people, and all of them were from Europe. The film was being primarily crafted at Prima Linea Productions in Angoulême, and another group of animators was working in the Hungarian studio Kecskemétfilm. Why Not Productions in Paris was in charge of the overall production. *The Red Turtle* took three years to make, longer than the usual length of time required for an animated feature. Luckily enough, the producers understood Dudok de Wit's indispensable need for time, surrounded by a tight-knit group of trusted collaborators. "If you have a really large team, the style of the film gets watered down. As a director, I wouldn't have the time to channel the entire animation in the right direction",[20] explained the filmmaker.

Ultimately, each one of *The Red Turtle*'s 650 scenes emerged from daily debates with his carefully selected team of specialists. For the first time in his life, Dudok de Wit did not animate his film. His role was to steer the group and make sure they followed his guidelines with regards to the film's coherence, both in terms of style and language. "I was always with them, all the time in the same building. It was very important for me to have that energy and resonance and close chemistry with them",[20] said the filmmaker. Animation clean-up supervisor Marie Bouchet stressed the importance of that energy on a human level:

> The main quality of Michael's way of directing was his sincere care for everyone who worked on the film. He often kept telling us how grateful he was. This instilled an amazing energy to the whole team who would bring out their best in the work.[21]

Animator Paul Williams appreciated very much Dudok de Wit's "sense of empathy that connects the artist to the person, rather than the artist to the worker".[22]

But, for the filmmaker, it was also relentless:

> All day long, every day, every week, every month, every year. When you're not used to that, when you're mostly an animator sitting alone, sometimes in silence, for long periods of time, just animating by yourself or drawing backgrounds, or the storyboard ... to bounce from that to talking non-stop with the team, that was a big jump for me.[23]

He was extremely mindful of his collaborators' sensibility, as he himself was all too aware of animators' frustration with the strict hierarchical system of the larger studios.

"Every animator was different, with a unique approach, and I wanted to understand this really well", observed Dudok de Wit.

> I wanted to allow each person a relative artistic freedom, within the parameters of the project of course, and then worry about things such as the overall quality being high enough, or whether the audience will empathize with the characters.[2]

Animator Paul Williams, who assisted other animators in helping them to refine certain sequences in *The Red Turtle*, confirmed filmmaker's

> emphasis on feeling and sensibility which for me was a key part of the film. As an animator I can sometimes get caught up in the mechanics of an action, seeing only the moment rather than the fuller, larger picture. For example when animating a scene I would usually consider mostly the scenes hooking up (before and after) and its place in the sequence. Whereas my job on *The Red Turtle* was more about the sensibility of a scene within that sequence and the moment in terms of the pacing of the sequence and its place in the film. Often, I would have to fix mechanical issues as well, but ultimately it always had to "feel right" for that moment in the movie.[24]

A weekly screening of the most recently validated sections quickly became an important ritual for the team. Sharing the same building and constantly exchanging ideas resulted in a homogeneous "Dudok de Wit" visual style that would slightly shift and evolve throughout production.

The Red Turtle was released in 2016 and distributed all over the world, except in China. It was premiered during the Cannes Film Festival in June 2016, where it won the *Un Certain Regard* Special Jury Prize. That same year, the film opened the Annecy Film Festival. In 2017, the feature was nominated for the Academy Award, won the Annie Award for the Best Independent

Animated Feature and swept numerous awards in various film festivals all over the world (Zagreb, Hiroshima).

6.4 THE ART OF ANIMATION

Striving to find the right quality of line and a proper animation style, Dudok de Wit and the team started the first animation tests by drawing with pencil on paper. But then, in September 2011, the filmmaker visited the studio Prima Linea Productions in Angouleme, where he was invited to see the final phase of the feature *Wolfy, the Incredible Secret*,[25] drawn entirely on Cintiq tablets. Comparing the test result of a hand-drawn 2D animation with that of a TV Paint Software on Cintiq tablet, Dudok de Wit concluded that the latter was "more economical. It gave us more creative freedom and increased control for retouching. The line of the digital pencil was more beautiful and that convinced us".[13]

Two exceptional artists, Julien De Man and Eric Briche were, respectively, supervisors for background and layout. Huge, sensual, granitic rocks, white and fluffy or grey and heavy clouds, bamboo forests and mesmerizing starry nights have a delightful painterly look. An artisan quality of the landscapes was obtained through a grainy texture of the backgrounds, drawn with charcoal on paper with broad strokes, literally smudged with the palm of the hand, resulting in handcrafted quality. "The lines of the scanned backgrounds were done with pencil and paper. They were all combined and colored in Photoshop and compositing was done in Digital Fusion",[26] precised the filmmaker.

The special effects animation team, led by Mouloud Oussid, consisted of a dozen animators who worked on waves, backwashes, tsunami, storms and fire. In the course of production, the director only recommended small touch-ups on the scenery and animation, always bearing in mind the objectives he had set for himself from the very start:

> My first aim was to emphasize light and shadow, because I think it's graphically appealing and because it

reinforces the relationship between the animation and the backgrounds. Another important aspect of our film's aesthetics, for me, was in maintaining a sense of simplicity throughout. The team purposefully ensured they never saturated the entire frame with details and would select only one or two dominant colours per sequence. As for the animation, my choice was to go for relatively realistic design and movement. That was very ambitious because it's one of the most difficult approaches to an animated film.[27]

The colour research team, supervised by Emma McCann for the animation and Julien de Man for the backgrounds, was responsible for the continuity and harmony of colours. One of the interesting examples of colour problem solving is demonstrated in the night sequences which were originally in black and grey tones, free of any colour. During the final colour adjustment sessions, the colour grader noticed that the black and grey effect did not feel entirely right in the night sequences, because the effect appeared too suddenly. He suggested inserting a subtle deep blue colour at the beginning of each nocturnal sequence and reducing the blue gradually and almost invisibly to zero over the next ten seconds or so, arriving at the desired black and grey ambiance. This worked well.[28] Before creating the final artwork of the film, it was first necessary to establish the choice of colours and for that reason a simplified image of each scene was created to establish the right palette. There were about 650 scenes. The alignment of these images, called the colour board, allowed us to check the rhythm and the balance of colours,[29] explained Dudok de Wit.

The majestic orange–red fire scene was added both for the purpose of the story and to introduce a splash of warm colours in an otherwise grey–brown colour palette in that section of the film. The role of colour as an emotional conveyor is best illustrated in the sequence of the enraged main character, after the turtle has destroyed his raft for the third time. In an evocative sunset mise-en-scène, his anger was visually emphasised by the spectrum of potent scarlet-red and orange colours. The transparency of green each hour of day, the translucency of light blue just under the surface of the ocean, the opacity of grey in the moonlight scenes, the saffron golden light on the gentle slopes of the grassy confines of the island, the melancholy blue of the evening sky - one could easily guess the time of day by merely observing the intensity of light in the sequences of *The Red Turtle*. Whilst admiring the atmospheres in the films' landscapes, the light and colours that shaped them, I was reminded of Henri Focillon[30] and the way he used to describe landscapes in the paintings of the Italian renaissance painter Piero della Francesca:

> The landscape, as an image of the world, is no longer just a background but an "ambience". It is not a mise-en-scène, it is a place in the mind. It is neither abstract nor imaginary, but it is neither a mere observation of reality.[31]

The raft, turtles and some of the ocean waves were digitally animated. The turtle was particularly hard to animate, because of its slowness and the complex pattern on its carapace and legs. To avoid any wobbling effects or, even worse, pointless stylisation, digital animation was used. The turtle's shell texture was created in Photoshop and placated onto the character using Blackmagic Design's Fusion. The Belgian animator Dominique Gantois, who animated the turtle, dives in his spare time and understands water and the natural movements of the water creature.

But the hardest part for the animators was "to recreate the projected shadows that follow the curves of each bamboo shaft and must be animated manually",[32] said animation supervisor Jean-Christophe Lie.

Simulating water was another difficult challenge for the animators at Prima Linea in Angouleme. Water is lively, transparent and reflective, and animators had to stylise it. Yet, they had to be very cautious in this process because to overstylise meant to lose the magic of water. Dudok de Wit explained that water for him is opaque and mysterious at the same time:

> It has a closed surface and you can't see underneath and the film used that a lot. Sometimes it has reflective qualities. When you see the man moving and you have a mirror image moving in synchronization, it's very pleasant, on a subtle level. It is a bit like seeing two synchronized dancers instead of one. But unlike my short films, *The Red Turtle* didn't explore reflection that often, because the surface was not always tranquil enough. There is also the effect of the crystal-clear transparency under water, which is very attractive. In those moments the film plays with the magic of floating in a seemingly empty space.[33]

Dudok de Wit never uses rotoscoping techniques in his films. Instead, he filmed live action sequences, and the footage of the actors only served as a reference point for animators. Animation supervisor Jean-Christophe Lie explained: "We used analytic animation. Actors were filmed and their strongest poses were isolated. The camera angles were readapted in the layout, then everything was redrawn, as one would do in a life drawing class".[32] Before production started, the filmmaker spent ten days researching on one of the Seychelles islands, living with the local people and accumulating visual material that would be used by the artists during production. Waves, backwashes, clouds, light, granite rocks, vegetation, animals – everything was meticulously filmed and photographed by the filmmaker.

"When characters express themselves emotionally, their body language can be really eloquent",[2] observed the filmmaker. In search of inspiration, he watched performances of modern dance where choreography and flux of movements can have a strong effect on our sensibility. The main character is immersed in Nature. He belongs there, he is a part of it. We don't need to see his face to be emotionally involved; acting, music and animation are expressive enough. The filmmaker candidly admits that he can be genuinely moved by the expression of the actors' faces in live-action films' close-ups but that he prefers not to use the close-up technique in his films.[34] In *The Red Turtle*, he insisted on relying on body movement to convey emotions:

> In animation, the common practice is to convey emotions mainly through facial expressions and through the gestures of the arms and the hands, but we can convey them of course through the behaviour of the whole body, the way people stand somewhere, or lie down. I really like simple, natural body language when we use this realistic animation style. The face, in general, is very complex and I prefer not to zoom into it too much because in animation a close-up can reveal an over-simplified face and the eyes for instance can be too graphic.[2]

Jean-Christophe Lie concurred: "Michael had taken a firm stance: not to give in to emotion triggered by music. He wanted the gestures, first and foremost, to inspire emotion".[32]

Occasionally though, a few scenes in the film do show the characters from close range, albeit in profile (for instance, in the night scene with the desperate, sick castaway under the timeless starry sky). The outline of the man's face and his actual features appears very clearly. Dudok de Wit is a strong believer in these small details and, in his perfectionism, often pushes their boundaries. Convinced that spectators need these extra visual pieces of information and that they can see more, on a subconscious level, than they realise, the camera lingers for a while on the profile of the protagonists' hands, whose gestures bring out a sense of interlacing emotion and elegance. This artistic credo is no better illustrated than in the sublime underwater dancing scene where the woman and man explore and experience each other. In this Pina Bausch-like choreography of pas de deux, the movements of the two bodies and their hands produce a rapturing effect on the spectator.

Dudok de Wit understands that hand gestures can sometimes be more powerful than facial expressions. The nocturnal scene with the couple standing in profile against the boundless sky perforated by stars is particularly touching, in no small part thanks to the mere hand gestures. The man is haunted by a sense of guilt for having killed the red turtle, and the mute flashbacks of that painful event add a strong dose of anxiety to the scene. Finally, in an act of forgiveness, the woman slowly touches the man's forehead with her fingers. He immediately closes his eyes as if he had been waiting for that healing gesture all along. The absence of music is a very astute choice for this scene: the slow breathing of the characters and the nightly sounds of nature attest that they are not in a dream. The poetic quality of the scene also lies in the beauty of the drawing, the fluidity of the animation and the serenity of the pace.

Another vivid and poignant scene bare of musical score is the one in which the son announces to his parents his decision to leave. The evocative force of this sequence rests essentially on the convincing acting of the protagonists, their mute gestures and the silent geometry of their stares. The only perceived sound is the mother's deep and dismayed sigh in the midst of the indifferent night. The following sequence depicts the harmonious tableau of three bodies lying close to each other in the grass. The mother is next to the son but lies slightly closer to her companion. Before going to sleep, she gently lays her hand over her son's, and soon after, he repays the courtesy by reciprocating the gesture. The scene closes with the slow flight of a large seabird against the backdrop of the nightly sky.

The animation is smooth, fluid, organic, light and fresh. The quiet oneiric scenes are visually captivating and are perfectly juxtaposed to the more dynamic sequences, such as the one of the tsunami for example. The realistic animation of clothes or leaves, gently blown by the wind, of a woman's hair under the water, the allegorical love dance of the couple in the sky at night – those are true gems of this art.

6.5 THE WORLD OF ELEGANCE, PRECISION AND EMOTION

The visual language of *The Red Turtle* reflects the filmmaker's unique graphic style, forged through years of joyful and elegant animation. Most of the visual characteristics of this film are to be found in his short films, his commercial works and his book illustrations for children. A recurring theme running through all his short films is the idea of a separation that ends in a harmonious union and the simplicity of that seamless union. Fond of the motto that "less is more", the director is seen to apply this principle in the simplicity of his drawings: the sleek, secure, sometimes trembling, always elegant pencil line or the thick brush organic line is his trademark. His characters are recognizable by their stylised faces and slender body contours, framed by a thick shadow. The characters, perfectly integrated to the background, express themselves mainly through body language. Close-ups are inexistent, whilst long takes are ever present; landscape and a nature-inspired colour palette, along with the musical score, act as strong emotional vectors.

Dudok de Wit's films are unmistakably recognisable by the omnipresence of shadows, which serve his dynamic use of light. The filmmaker finds it graphically interesting to play with the shadows formed both by direct and indirect light. Characters walking through the shadows under the sun- or moonlight are of utmost interest to him. The vertical row of elongated, black shadows of bamboo stems in the scene of the son's restless night before his departure certainly infuses it with added dramatic effect. Beautiful reflections on the surface of the water had to be synchronised with the movements of the characters. The filmmaker observed that the slight shadow line of the waves and backwashes was necessary in order to avoid them looking too abstract.[35] All the shadows were already referenced in his initial *The Red Turtle* storyboard, and the main task of the small group of "shadow animators", guided by Pascal Herbreteau, was to interpret them in his unique style.

Clouds are present in every Dudok de Wit's film: in *The Monk and the Fish*, they have the lightness of a watercolour layer; in *Father and Daughter*, their monochrome, artisan quality adds to the air of nostalgia. In *The Red Turtle*, clouds stand as key protagonists in the lavishly executed backgrounds. An artist of great sensibility, background supervisor Julian De Man recalls that the biggest challenge for him whilst working on backgrounds was precisely the clouds:

> Clouds are special. Clouds can take so many different forms and, depending on the person, can make you feel so many different things. For me, it is probably the most sensitive thing to represent in a background. I loved clouds before *The Red Turtle*, and I love them even more now. I know Michael loves them too, and the backgrounds with clouds were actually the ones he spent most of his time on.[36]

The recurrent visual motif of *The Red Turtle* is a curve. When Dudok de Wit met the Studio Ghibli producers for the first time in Tokyo, he helped himself to a large calligraphy brush lying on the table and a piece of paper, and he painted a simple, curved ink line. Nature's curves (in the beach line, the shape of the stones, the trees) confer a certain visual coherence to the film. This idea of the natural origins of the curved line points to his long-held admiration and profound reverence for Japanese calligraphy. *The Aroma of Tea*, for instance, clearly bears the mark of this source of inspiration. He singled out, in particular, the drawings of a Japanese Zen Buddhist monk Hakuin Ekaku (1686–1768) that touched him deeply.

> My visual creativity changed when I saw Hakuin's paintings in a book about Zen art. His sense of space and the elegance of his line ... Since discovering Hakuin's unique harmony between maturity and simplicity, I have been inspired to search for that unique harmony myself.[37]

Diagonal lines dominate the film as they contribute to the continuity between the scenes and are, once again, typical of Dudok de Wit's scene compositions. Diagonals create dynamism and the necessary energetic drive in this otherwise slow, meditative feature. It may not be noticeable at first, but the movement of the camera following the character's glance is one invisible, diagonal line. In some sequences, the filmmaker chose to rotate the camera gently around the subject. The fluid camera movements in *The Red Turtle* include high-angle shots, as well as particular low angles he much admires in some of Terrence Malick's films.[38]

The physiognomy of the castaway in *The Red Turtle* shares a resemblance with the Captain Haddock's face, while his eyes resemble Tintin's eyes, the two adventurous characters from the series of the Tintin comic books by Belgian author Georges Remi known as Hergé (1907–1983). His body language is that of a common, vigorous man, with calm and assured movements. His hands are not particularly elegant; his arms are sturdy. The woman, on the other side, was a more challenging type to animate: Dudok de Wit didn't want her manners to be associated with a specific culture or education. The woman, the epitome of the mystery of transformation and magic, was intended to be as simple and lively as Nature itself. "It was a real challenge to invent the figure of the woman because her physical stature had to be more subtle and delicate than the rest of the characters in our film, her face in particular",[39] explained the filmmaker. The character of the little boy, the couple's son, was another challenging task for the animators: his bouncy movements in the scene where he discovers the bottle in the sea are reminiscent of those of the agitated monk in his previous short *The Monk and the Fish*.

Certain landscape details (the shape of the trees, the density of the foliage), several iconographical scene solutions and the quiet narrative pace of the story could possibly have been inspired by one of Dudok de Wit's favuorite comic books *The Walking Man*, by Japanese manga artist Jiro Taniguchi (1947–2017). This graphic novel with scant dialogues fascinated him to such an extent that he even briefly considered adapting the book into an animated film. Charmed by Taniguchi's effective and economic graphic language, which borrowed heavily from the European comic tradition, he fell for the simplicity of the story and its composition structure.[40] The scene in which the sick castaway lies asleep on his back on the bed of leaves, in the bamboo forest, brings to mind a similar image of Taniguchi's walking man, resting under the tree on the bed of cherry flowers. Not only is the position of their bodies similar, but both authors choose to zoom on the hands of their protagonists, with the intention of visually emphasising and communicating the softness of the natural material under their palms.

The representation of cyclical time was something that the filmmaker had already grappled with in his Oscar-winning short *Father and Daughter*. Human beings are generally touched by the cycles of life because they remind us of our mortality.

"I find life cycles very beautiful", said Dudok de Wit. "I get moved by the idea of generations succeeding each other. When I see that in different contexts, in photos or novels, I find it incredibly affecting. I wanted to play with that in the film".[41] The raw truth at the heart of the cycle of life is represented in the playful (the effect of the music marvelously contradicts the subject matter) beach scene in which the couple's toddler tries to taste a little crab and immediately spits it out, only for a seagull to swiftly catch it and fly away with it. These couple of seconds demonstrate the director's "feel for the comedy of small animals"[20] as well as "the ironic side of his humour, a kind of irony wrapped in innocence".[42]

Dudok de Wit says he likes timelessness. *The Red Turtle* is a timeless film in two ways at least: we cannot distinguish the period in which the story is set, and we are left guessing about the previous life of the main character. The film contains yet another quality of timelessness, one in which time stands still: "When you are concentrated on something or when you are attracted to something extremely beautiful, that's when the past and future are not important",[43] observed the filmmaker. The feeling of timelessness in this feature results from a perfect combination between the representations of nature (the vast landscapes with wide-open horizons, the plants and animals, the transparency of water), the sounds of nature and the musical score. Timeless are the characters and their natural movements; timeless is the simplicity of their way of life.

6.6 THE SCORE – SOUNDS OF THE FILM AND THE MUSIC THAT SOUND LIKE ONE

During the making of the film, Dudok de Wit was concerned about the absence of any ideas regarding the music. Whilst working on his previous short films, he had always had the score in advance or at least an idea of the musical arrangement. The line producers of *The Red Turtle*, Christophe Jankovic and Valerie Shermann, presented him to French composer Laurent Perez del Mar,[44] who had written the scores of the animated features their studio had produced in the past.[45] The composer joined the production of *The Red Turtle* when the film was already in the editing phase, and he was given a challenging two months till deadline.

I didn't have a clear idea of a specific musical style. Laurent Perez del Mar made a few suggestions, including a very beautiful melody that was perfect for the main theme. I was delighted. He was quick to suggest music where I would not have thought having any, and he was right. He often surprised me,[13] recalled Dudok de Wit.

"Michael just made a very simple request: 'I want a cello, a ternary rhythm and synthetic textures. I don't want a piano'",[46] Perez del Mar told me in an interview.

Described by numerous film critics as subtle, unobtrusive, stunning, mesmerizing, captivating, the score for *The Red Turtle* is its pulsating heart. The French composer was given complete freedom to compose the music and, as far as he is concerned, it turned out to be a pure, intuitive experience. Respect for silence and the sounds of nature, harmony between the music, the sounds and the natural ambience, and a musical rhythm that would seamlessly slide into the narrative were the key guiding principles for Perez del Mar.

However, *The Red Turtle* feature is equally singular by its long absences of music (the contrast between the roaring scenes of the storm or tsunami and the diegetic silence of the island's hinterland), and the composer intuitively understood that not every emotion of the characters needed to be underlined musically. Curiously enough, this "absence of music" was also noted by animation historian Giannalberto Bendazzi who observed that, in *The Red Turtle*: "there are no dialogues; there is no music. There are only sounds",[47] hence confirming the saying that the best film music is the inaudible one.[48]

Perez del Mar's score for *The Red Turtle* is far for being inaudible of course. The music is present in half of the film's duration and consists of soprano parts, rich orchestral arrangements, refined string pieces (cello, violin) and pulsing percussions (percussive bamboo and foliage create "natural sonority and wooden textures"[49]). The score grows progressively within the frame of the film: its light and quiet presence, at the beginning, transforms into powerful crescendos when strong and dramatic narrative moments start to unfold. The tsunami scene is particularly fierce and arresting, thanks, in part, to the perfectly accurate blend of natural sounds and music. In the final stage of post-production, it was decided that music and sounds would be mixed simultaneously in order to preserve a certain coherence between the two.[50] Music leads the spectator through the scenes: it enriches the narrative by expressing spiritual moods of isolation and yearning. It also plays the role of emotion signifier (melancholia, sadness, solitude, moments of happiness) and serves to amplify continuity and underpin the rhythm of the film.

While composing for the feature, Perez del Mar mainly drew his inspiration from the images of the film and discussions with Dudok de Wit: "We never talked about instruments or orchestration, we just focused on emotions. When you have such incredible images in front of your eyes, inspiration is never far away". The composer's major challenge was to find the right musical rhythm that would "respect the silences and nature's sounds, whilst bringing a true added layer of emotion throughout the narrative". In order to obtain the soundtrack's coherence, he collaborated closely with the sound supervisor Bruno Seznec and Sébastien Marquilly and the sound mixer Fabien Devillers at Piste Rouge, Paris. The colours of the music add a quality of timelessness and the "third dimension"[51] to the film. (Music channels what cannot be seen in images.)

Instrumental combinations affect the development of the theme. For example, Perez del Mar accentuated the presence of a strong female character by introducing soprano solos. In general, the composer uses a human voice:

> before as an instrument in an abstract way, when the situations are beyond us, when we touch something almost mystical. In *The Red Turtle*, I used it at a point when life was being created, during the love scene allegory between the two protagonists.[52]

The playful flute melody rises on the son's arrival and in the scenes of his childhood. Monochromes, night scenes and those linked to emotions of fear and sense of anxiety are often backed by a powerful ensemble of string instruments (violin, viola, cello). The main musical theme originates from (and underscores) a scene where the castaway, flying over the never-ending wooden pier, dreams of his final escape from the island. In order to heighten the presence of water in the film, the composer came up with a peculiar combination of orchestra strings and analog textures.

In 2017, with *The Red Turtle* score, described as "frequently extremely beautiful, full of emotion" and a music that "moves the heart with the utmost sincerity",[53] Perez del Mar won the award for the Best Original Score for an Animated Feature by the International Film Music Critics Association.

6.7 ABOUT A PROVERBIAL DUDOK DE WIT'S PERFECTIONISM

"I don't really believe in making a perfect film but working towards perfection is exciting enough for me. I have learnt to accept imperfection", said the filmmaker in his Venetian masterclass in December 2017. Working towards perfection means dissatisfaction with the result obtained because it could always be improved. Working towards perfection means adding a detail to the landscape that could make a difference for a more attentive spectator (but, more likely, for the own joy and satisfaction of its creator). Although Dudok de Wit was supported by a team of very talented artists, he would usually retouch some details of the backgrounds on weekends. For the filmmaker it was

> the question of the codes and of the personal taste. In some scenes I thought the light could be even more interesting. Obviously, it was not a question of modifying the angle of the light but rather its colour: was it necessary to put a lot of shadows, or reduce them, or make them in contrast or even softer? Would we be polishing the light that falls on the tree trunks, knowing that it takes time, or was it not worth it? For each of my films, I keep looking for things and retouch elements until the very end. And on *The Red Turtle* even more than ever! Despite our cohesion, we were a team with very different artistic sensitivities, so in the end there was still a lot to retouch.[54]

Working towards perfection also means striving to animate the gait of a female protagonist so as to evoke a form of primordial femininity rather than the swaying strides of a modern, contemporary woman. The sound of the water drops falling from the broken bamboo stem after the tsunami disaster, the son's mesmerizing dream in which he appears immersed up to the waist on the top of a gigantic gelatinous wave and the meticulous drawing of a millipede or every tiny leave fluttering in the wind – they all display the director's unquenchable thirst for a perfect film. "He is in constant search of perfection", said one of the animators in the Dutch documentary film *The Longing of Michael Dudok de Wit*. "He is like a child with his head in the clouds".[55] The Prima Linea line producers remember "Michael's perfectionism and how his outlook embraces all aspects of the film, right down to the tiniest details",[56] whereas the animation supervisor, Jean-Christophe Lie, observed: "He is probably one of the greatest perfectionists I have met. But he's very open to different points of view, and that's very stimulating".[32] Background supervisor Julien De Man rightly noted:

> During the film production, Michael was ever-present, he almost lived in the studio. Long days, short nights, short weekends. He was there, sometimes very tired but always happy, available and very involved. Always questioning, never sure of anything because always on the quest for perfection. He had to vet every little thing, change design of a shell on the sand, dots in the texture of the sky, tint of the sea, shape of the clouds, hair of the character. He checked every stage of the film, every pixel of every background. In detail and taking the time he needed. And I think that is what makes the difference and gives a visual coherence to the whole film.[57]

In truth, Dudok de Wit's working method is equally pivotal to making the difference and forging the way towards a true work of art. The idiosyncratic mixture of intuition and rationality prevents his quest for perfection from becoming sterile and self-referential and enables it to propel his art. "A good film can be acceptable, but I want ours to be a fantastic one and I use every free moment to improve the film",[58] concluded the filmmaker.

6.8 THE VOICES OF SOME CRITICS

> The archetype is a force, it has autonomy. It can certainly seize you.[59]

> CARL GUSTAV JUNG

Animation historian Giannalberto Bendazzi described the "cinematographic art" of *The Red Turtle* as a "highly humanist audiovisual art in the most sincere and best sense".[60]

The director and reputed perfectionist, co-founder of the Ghibli Studio, Hayao Miyazaki, gave his opinion on *The Red Turtle* in an informal talk with Dudok de Wit: "It's marvelous that the film is absolutely free of influences from Japanese animation". Adding, in his ambiguous way, "I want the staff from this movie. If I had this staff (*The Red Turtle* staff), I think I could do it...".[61]

Dudok de Wit simply couldn't have received a bigger compliment from the director of *Spirited Away*: he had always deeply admired Studio Ghibli films and was influenced by their graphic style "on a subconscious level".[62]

In 2004, after the Seoul screening of Dudok de Wit's short *The Aroma of Tea*, Isao Takahata revealed that he had invited the director "to create a film based on symbolism, not on abstraction".[63] It is highly probable that, around that time, he came up with the idea of an artistic collaboration with the Dutch filmmaker. Takahata noticed a few similarities in their respective graphic styles: lots of white space on the screen (in order to stimulate the audience's imagination) and simple animation that never loses its sense of the real. Takahata added that he felt "empathy with Dudok de Wit's somewhat Eastern view of nature".[63] Indeed, many of his details of nature (the vegetation, seashells, algae, insects, birds) are evocative of Ukiyo-e painters' style. On the other hand, the backgrounds in *The Red Turtle* were executed in a pure "Dudok de Wit" European genre: the vast skies and the horizon, flying birds and Vermeer-esque clouds in all their granulated charcoal quality texture are resolutely the filmmaker's trademark, dating back to his watercolour film *The Monk and the Fish* and a charcoal technique delight in *Father and Daughter*.

The Red Turtle's timing has the quiet rhythm of human breathing. It has a silent, meditative quality in the oneiric, monochrome night scenes or in those imbued with the power of filmmaker's graphic language, filled with the echoes of natural sounds and human voices that induce empathy. Still, the film also contains its inner dynamism in the representations of untamable forces of nature in its eternal evolving (opening storm scene), conveyed in the beautiful drawings and superb animation and accentuated by the score.

In the manual for students of the history of animation, key points of Bendazzi's critical analyses of Miyazaki's and Takahata's body of work apply perfectly to Dudok de Wit's ouevre.[64] In the chapter dedicated to Isao Takahata, "a filmmaker of the human dignity", Bendazzi concludes:

> Takahata doesn't treat realism like a sterile imitation of appearances, he doesn't exclude from it a comedic quality, poetry or oneirism. Nevertheless, each one of these motifs derives from reality: they emerge from everyday life and from its staunchly documented observation.[65]

Similarly, in the chapter on Hayao Miyazaki's work, Bendazzi observed that

> ... Miyazaki inserts in his films characters and sentiments, clear plots, a fanatical love for details and a steadfast spirit of respect for nature and for his fellow human beings. His style is that of a Maestro, pleasant and powerful. His films reflect the power of a person who has passion inside and a proper voice to express it.[66]

An animated hymn to Life, *The Red Turtle* is Dudok de Wit's coming of age as an author. This feature is like a precious multifaceted gem that can be admired from different angles and will resonate differently with each spectator. Depending on the intensity of the light and the angle of the viewing, it will reveal the goldsmith's exquisite cutting and polishing ability. *The Red Turtle*, as a perfect union of formal (drawing, colour, composition) and film language elements (animation, timing, editing, sounds, music) clearly demonstrates the author's reverence for nature and his deep respect for human beings. Throughout the narrative flow, the spectator gets emotionally exposed to a number of archetypes (birth, mother, death, love, father–son relationship) and their images (dreams, fantasies).[67] The stylistic and narrative coherence of this "quietly groundbreaking"[68] quality in *The Red Turtle* stemmed from the director's long years of animation experience and the authentic inspiration he drew from the best Studio Ghibli films. This visually distilled and wordless film could also be seen as homage to the Japanese classical culture in general, as evidenced in its representation of nature or the rarefied haiku atmosphere of certain of its scenes. Conversely, this work is also deeply rooted in the best European artistic tradition.

And what about the message of the film? Dudok de Wit, the man who succeeded in animating the feeling of longing, once said that all his films were quite simple and didn't carry any philosophical messages. About *The Red Turtle* though, he suggested it could be seen "as a film about self-discovery. Life is a path towards the discovery of maturity for oneself and the simplicity behind the apparent complexity of things".[69] We finally might push a big sigh of relief if we accept the filmmaker's following idea: "When we have a strong identification with nature, we don't say anymore 'I'm here and death is over there', but rather 'I'm life and I'm death', then there is no conflict".[70] Could this simple message be consolatory and eye-opening enough for us? In the first part of the film, in which the main character is alone in nature and strives to escape his crushing solitude, questions keep emerging: Who are we when we do not have society to reflect ourselves in? How would I cope with this isolation if I were there? Maybe Dudok de Wit's films don't have messages, but they certainly bring out questions, and they certainly have purposes. They make us think. They trigger emotions. They make us cry. They stir us deeply. They give us hope.

One gloomy December afternoon in Venice, Italy, during his masterclass in the Academy of Arts, he confided to a group of students:

Looking at life in general I found out that all its finest qualities have to do with sensitivity: empathy, compassion, love, trust, deep gratitude and so on. I suppose the purpose of this film is to remind the spectators of their sensitivity, to remind them how wonderful sensitivity is.

NOTES

1. Kitson, Clare, *Yuri Norstein and Tale of Tales: An Animator's Journey*, Indiana University Press, Bloomington, 2005, p. 86.
2. Michael Dudok de Wit's email to Andrijana Ružić, 4 November 2019.
3. What added an "extra incentive to collaborating" were Dudok de Wit's long-term fascination for Japanese art and culture (calligraphy, haiku poetry, architecture, Zen Buddhism) and Studio Ghibli's founders' interest and curiosity in European culture in general.
4. McAllister, James, *Songs of the Sea. Exploring the Soundscape of The Red Turtle*, The London Economic, 25 September 2017, https://www.thelondoneconomic.com/film/songs-sea-exploring-soundscape-red-turtle/25/09/, retrieved 27 September 2017.
5. "Priča nije samo događaj, ona je pre svega izraz određenog životnog principa". in Sudović, Zlatko, Munitić, Ranko, *Zagrebački krug crtanog filma*, Vol. 4, p. 389, Zavod za kulturu Hrvatske, Zagreb, 1986. Ante Zaninović (1934) is a Croatian animator, director and screenplay writer from the famous Zagreb School of Animated Film. Translated from Croatian by Andrijana Ružić.
6. Digital Arts Staff, *Michael Dudok de Wit on Directing Studio Ghibli's New Film "The Red Turtle"*, 13 June 2017, https://www.digitalartsonline.co.uk/features/motion-graphics/interview-michael-dudok-de-wit-on-directing-studio-ghiblis-new-film-red-turtle/, retrieved 2 February 2018.
7. *Vier bevertjes en een kastanje*, Leopold, Amsterdam, 2007 and *Vier bevertjes in de nacht*, Leopold, Amsterdam, 2004 are Dudok de Wit's children's books available in Dutch, German and Korean language.
8. "I believe that I've become a filmmaker because I like telling stories. I consider myself rather a storyteller than an animator". Dudok de Wit in Kawa-Topor, Xavier, Nguyên, Ilan, *Michael*

Dudok de Wit. *Le cinéma d'animation sensible. Entretien avec le réalisateur de La Tortue Rouge,* Capricci, Paris, 2019, p. 140. Translated from French by Andrijana Ružić.

9. Studio Ghibli suggested Dudok de Wit a book written by Lafcadio Hearn, intitled *Kwaidan: Stories and Studies of Strange Things.* The book was published in 1903 and contains several Japanese ghost stories and a brief non-fiction study on insects.

10. Zhuo-Ning Su, *The Red Turtle director talks working with Studio Ghibli,* Storytelling Sans Dialogue and More, 17 October 2016, https://thefilmstage.com/features/the-red-turtle-director-talks-working-with-studio-ghibli-animating-sans-dialogue-more/, retrieved 3 December 2017.

11. Desowitz, Bill, *The Red Turtle: How the Animator Oscar Contender Handled Conflict,* IndieWire, 21 February 2017, http://www.indiewire.com/2017/02/the-red-turtle-oscar-video-1201785366/, retrieved 10 September 2017.

12. Why Not Productions producer Pascal Caucheteux invited Pascale Ferran (1960), a French director and scriptwriter, to help write the script with Dudok de Wit. Ferran's adaptation of the film she also directed, *Lady Chatterley* (2006), won several prestigious awards in France.

13. Genin, Bernard, *Interview with Michael Dudok de Wit,* Press Kit Wild Bunch. International Sales, https://www.wildbunch.biz/movie/the-red-turtle/, last retrieved 2 February 2018.

14. *Interview with Pascale Ferran,* Press Kit, Wild Bunch International Sales, https://www.wildbunch.biz/movie/the-red-turtle/, retrieved 2 February 2018.

15. Michael Dudok de Wit to Andrijana Ružić, London, 6 December 2018.

16. Céline Kélépikis's email to Andrijana Ružić, 25 March 2018.

17. Julien De Man's email to Andrijana Ružić, 9 April 2018.

18. Editor Céline Kélépikis helped him with the timing. Occasionally, storyboard artists would make their contribution and a producer took care of everyday matters.

19. Dudok de Wit's Masterclass, Venice Academy of Arts, December 2017.

20. Dudok de Wit, Alex, *Notes From a Small Island,* Sight and Sound, June 2017, http://www.primalinea.com/latortuerouge/revue-presse/Sight_Sound-1706.pdf, retrieved 10 March 2018.

21. Marie Bouchet's email to Andrijana Ružić, 2 April 2018.

22. Paul Williams's email to Andrijana Ružić, 24 September 2019.

23. Sarto, Dan, *Michael Dudok de Wit Talks "The Red Turtle" and Partnership with Studio Ghibli*, 10 February 2017, https://www. awn.com/animationworld/micha-l-dudok-de-wit-talks-red-turtle-and-partnership-studio-ghibli, retrieved 30 September 2017.
24. Paul Williams's email to Andrijana Ružić, 24 September 2019.
25. Directed by Eric Omond.
26. Sarto, Dan, *Michael Dudok de Wit Talks "The Red Turtle" and Partnership with Studio Ghibli*, 10 February 2017, https://www. awn.com/animationworld/micha-l-dudok-de-wit-talks-red-turtle-and-partnership-studio-ghibli, retrieved 30 September 2017.
27. Digital Arts Staff, *Michael Dudok de Wit on Directing Studio Ghibli's New Film "The Red Turtle"*, 13 June 2017, https://www. digitalartsonline.co.uk/features/motion-graphics/interview-michael-dudok-de-wit-on-directing-studio-ghiblis-new-film-red-turtle/, retrieved 2 February 2018.
28. This episode is often recounted by the filmmaker on his *The Red Turtle* masterclasses.
29. *La Tortue Rouge. Art book*, Wild Side, 2016, p. 36. Translated from French by Andrijana Ružić.
30. Henri Focillon (1881–1943) was a French art historian, theoretician of art, poet and a printmaker.
31. Focillon, Henri, *Piero della Francesca*, Abscondita, Milano, 2004, p. 118. Translated from Italian by Andrijana Ružić.
32. *Interview with Jean-Christophe Lie*, Press Kit, Wild Bunch International Sales, https://www.wildbunch.biz/movie/the-red-turtle/, retrieved 29 January 2018.
33. Michael Dudok de Wit's masterclass, Accademia di Belle Arti, Venezia, 2017.
34. Dudok de Wit explained in an interview with Andrijana Ružić that he is often inspired by live-action films. In this interview, he specifically mentioned two films he had recently seen that had particularly impressed him: *Gerry* (2002) by Gus Van Sant and *Son of Saul* (2015) by Laszlo Nemes. Zagreb/Mirogoj interview, June 2017.
35. Michael Dudok de Wit in VPRO Documentary film directed in 2016 by Thomas Doebele and Maarten Schmidt *Het Verlangen van Michael Dudok de Wit*.
36. From Julien De Man's email to Andrijana Ružić, 9 April 2018.
37. Dudok de Wit's Venice Academy of Arts Masterclass, December 2017.

38. Thomas, Lou, *The Red Turtle: The Films That Influenced Studio Ghibli's Latest Spellbinder*, BFI, 26 May 2017. http://www.bfi.org. uk/news-opinion/news-bfi/red-turtle-studio-ghibli-michael-dudok-wit-influences, retrieved 10 April 2018.
39. *La Tortue Rouge. Art Book.* West Side, 2016, p. 68. Translated from French by Andrijana Ružić.
40. *The Walking Man* tells the story of a man who observes and listens to the sounds of the anonymous suburban streets of Tokyo. Through the various seasons of the year, Taniguchi's walking man savours the small details of everyday life: the shape of a tree and its flowers in the spring, bird migrations, a starry night above his head while floating in the swimming pool, snowflakes on his face, the distorted vision through his broken spectacles. Now and again, it seems that time stands still for the walking man, that only the "here" and "now" exist. The mystery and magic hidden in the small things of life are only revealed to the eyes of the attentive observer.
41. Halfyard, Kurt, *Interview: The Red Turtle Director Michael Dudok de Wit Talks Studio Ghibli and More*, Screenanarchy, 26 January 2017, http://screenanarchy.com/2017/01/interview-the-red-turtle-director-michael-dudok-de-wit-talks-studio-ghibli-and-more.html, retrieved 10 April 2018.
42. Chief Assistant Animator Marie Bouchet, email to Andrijana Ružić, 2 April 2018.
43. Contender Conversations, YouTube, retrieved on 5 November 2017.
44. Born in Nice (1974) and based in Paris, Perez del Mar studied medicine and music and majored in music composition. His score for *The Red Turtle* has received numerous awards. Perez del Mar composes both for animated and feature films and is a member of the Academy of Motion Picture Arts and Science since 2017.
45. *Zarafa* (2012) and *Wolfy, The Incredible Secret* (2014).
46. Laurent Perez del Mar email to Andrijana Ružić, 27 July 2017. If not specified otherwise, the quotes by Perez del Mar derive from that mail.
47. Bendazzi, Giannalberto, *Animazione. Una storia globale*, Volume 2, UTET, Torino, 2017, p. 176. "Non ci sono parole, non c'è musica. Solo suoni". Translation from Italian to English by Andrijana Ružić.
48. More about rules of film music, see Chapter 4 in Gorbman, Claudia, *Unheard Melodies: Narrative Film Music*, BFI Publishing, Bloomington and Indiana University Press, London and Indiana, 1987.
49. Blondeau, Thomas, *Laurent Perez del Mar*, Ecran Total No. 1099, 29 June 2016.

50. *Interview with Laurent Perez del Mar*, Press Kit, Wild Bunch International Sales, https://www.wildbunch.biz/movie/the-red-turtle/, retrieved 10 February 2018. "The atmospheres, the wind, the birds, the music were all tuned up in their tonality. It made us feel like we had reached the very limits".

51. Interview with Laurent Perez del Mar, 13 December 2017, http://www.maisondelaradio.fr/article/une-musique-pour-loulou, retrieved 15 January 2018.

52. Schweiger, Daniel, *Interview with Laurent Perez del Mar*, Film Music Magazine, 20 March 2018 http://www.filmmusicmag.com/?p=18620, retrieved 21 March 2018.

53. Jon, *Laurent Perez del Mar receives IFMCA award for The Red Turtle*, http://filmmusiccritics.org/2017/03/laurent-perez-del-mar-receives-ifmca-award-for-the-red-turtle/, retrieved 2 November 2017.

54. Kawa-Topor, Xavier, Nguyên, Ilan, *Michael Dudok de Wit. Le cinéma d'animation sensible. Entretien avec le réalisateur de La Tortue Rouge*, Capricci, Paris, 2019, p. 98. Translated from French by Andrijana Ružić.

55. Michael Dudok de Wit in VPRO Documentary film directed in 2016 by Doebele Thomas and Schmidt Maarten *Het Verlangen van Michael Dudok de Wit*.

56. *Interview with* Prima Linea, Press Kit, Wild Bunch International Sales, https://www.wildbunch.biz/movie/the-red-turtle/, retrieved 29 January 2018.

57. Julien De Man email to Andrijana Ružić, 9 April 2018.

58. Michael Dudok de Wit in VPRO Documentary film directed in 2016 by Doebele Thomas and Schmidt Maarten *Het Verlangen van Michael Dudok de Wit*.

59. Excerpt from Carl Gustav Jung's interview in Mark Whitney's documentary *Matter of Heart* (1983), https://www.youtube.com/watch?v=lxXyTrdgJKg&index=1&list=FLHaRozXuHcnLE8UCP4mQXPg&t=1984s, retrieved in 15 February 2018.

60. Bendazzi, Giannalberto, *Animazione. Una storia globale*, Volume 2, UTET, Milano, 2017, p. 176. Translation from Italian by Andrijana Ružić.

61. Baseel, Casey, *Hayao Miyazaki slams anime, hints at comeback, and praises The Red Turtle, all in one breath*, SoraNews24, 2 September 2016, https://en.rocketnews24.com/2016/09/02/hayao-miyazaki-slams-anime-hints-at-comeback-and-praises-the-red-turtle-and-all-in-one-breath/, retrieved 10 February 2018.

62. Loughrey, Clarisse, *The Red Turtle: Director Michael Dudok de Wit on his unique collaboration with the Studio Ghibli*, Independent, 30 May 2017, http://www.independent.co.uk/arts-entertainment/films/features/the-red-turtle-studio-ghibli-michael-dudok-de-wit-interview-animation-cannes-2016-release-date-a7763506.html, retrieved 10 February 2018.

63. *Interview with Isao Takahata*, Press Kit, Wild Bunch International Sales, https://www.wildbunch.biz/movie/the-red-turtle/, retrieved 10 February 2018.

64. Bendazzi, Giannalberto, *Lezioni sul cinema d'animazione*, CUEM, Milano, 2004. Translated from Italian by Andrijana Ružić.

65. Bendazzi, Giannalberto, *Lezioni sul cinema d'animazione*, CUEM, Milano, 2004, p. 149. Translated from Italian by Andrijana Ružić.

66. Bendazzi, Giannalberto, *Lezioni sul cinema d'animazione*, CUEM, Milano, 2004, p. 153. Translated from Italian by Andrijana Ružić.

67. According to Jung, archetypal or primordial images, as innate tendencies which shape human behavior, "derive from the repeated observation that myths and universal literature stories contain well defined themes which appear every time and everywhere. We often meet these themes in the fantasies, dreams, delirious ideas and illusions of persons living nowadays". These themes are based on archetypes. They impress, influence and fascinate us by arousing deep and intense emotions. *Concept of Archetypes at Carl Jung* in Carl Jung Resources http://www.carljung.net/archetypes.html, retrieved on 30 March 2018.

68. Fear, David, *Rolling Stone*, 23 January 2017, http://www.rollingstone.com/movies/reviews/the-red-turtle-movie-review-w461064, retrieved 5 November 2017.

69. Kawa-Topor, Xavier, Nguyên, Ilan, *Michael Dudok de Wit. Le cinéma d'animation sensible. Entretien avec le réalisa-teur de La Tortue Rouge*, Capricci, Paris, 2019, p. 121. Translated from French by Andrijana Ružić.

70. Michael Dudok de Wit in VPRO Documentary film directed in 2016 by Doebele Thomas and Schmidt Maarten *Het Verlangen van Michael Dudok de Wit*.

Epilogue

Yuri Norstein about Michael Dudok de Wit's Films

I heard about Michael Dudok de Wit for the first time from my wife Francesca Yarbusova.[1] Back in the nineties, she participated at the Leipzig film festival as a jury member. When she returned home, she told me that she particularly liked one film, simply a masterpiece, called *The Monk and the Fish*.

A few years later, in Russia, at the festival in Tarusa, Dudok de Wit's film *Father and Daughter* was screened. That film struck me. It was just wonderful from all points of view. I liked its overall simplicity: it was simple in the composition, in the clarity of action and animation. The editing was wonderful and subtle, and music sounded good there; it reminded me of Amur melody.[2]

Many years later, *The Red Turtle* appeared. I understood that the Japanese were the co-producers, and I can see clearly why. Because in terms of rhythm, calmness, long elaboration of episodes, attention to a detail, it is absolutely a Japanese film. There is the principle of uncertainty and mystery. At the same time, this film is deeply philosophical. In this sense, in Japan, China and in the East, in general, everything, even in everyday life, is a subject to a completely defined and very well-developed philosophy of art. Here it's probably good to recall these wonderful lines of vastness and deep philosophy of one Japanese poet,[3] just three lines:

And what is it, the heart?
It is the sound of the pine breeze
There in the sumi-e.

Sumi-e[4] is a kind of a graphic space. And the sound of a pine – there the author wants to convey something that cannot be described. And Michael Dudok de Wit does the same. A lot of similar things went into his films simultaneously.

Yuri Norstein,
Moscow, 19 October 2019

NOTES

1 Spouse of Yuri Norstein, Francesca Yarbusova (1942), is the most talented Russian animation designer and the art director of all Norstein's short films.

2 A Russian waltz called *Waves of Amur.*

3 Zen Buddhist monk Ikkyu Zenji (1394–1481).

4 Sumi painting is Japanese ink painting originating from ancient China and is commonly described as a visually unadorned artwork, done in monochrome, with the use of (sumi) black ink and handmade paper. https://japanobjects.com/features/sumie, retrieved 30 November 2019.

Appendix 1

Glossary of Michael Dudok de Wit's Favourite Themes

T HIS GLOSSARY CONSISTS PRIMARILY of the pieces of a long conversation that has taken place in Dudok de Wit's studio in London, during several mild December days in 2018. The wooden shed studio is situated at the bottom of the backyard of the two-storey red-brick house, a typical residential construction in North London. The studio faces a very tidy lawn, lined up with several compost cases constructed by himself, a couple of young trees and a small bamboo angle. One old and very tall tree stands next to the kitchen window framed by the wreath of roses. Frantic squirrels run back and forth over the studio's roof. An extra bucolic taste to the picture is given by a small hole in the soil situated underneath the filmmaker's studio – a foxes' lair. "City foxes have a greyish fur, and they are not too shy. One day a cub showed up inside my studio, and it sat down near the door. I was sitting at my desk, and it just stared at me for a moment. As soon as I moved, it disappeared", laughs Dudok de Wit.

The small studio is luminous and very tidy. The classical animator's desk with wood framed lightbox is situated in the corner, below the window. The wide surface of an additional office desk is well divided: graphic pencils are gathered in pencil cup holders by their grade of thickness and a collection of carefully chosen Japanese painting brushes. The narrower walls are covered with reference books, personal archives and a small selection of filmmaker's books on various topics: nature, colours, travels, comics, favourite animation directors, animals. There is a dozen of books only on bamboos and trees. The framed Rembrandt's copy of *The Three Trees* etching from his childhood's bedroom found its place above the highest library shelf. The wider walls are pinned with posters, reference photographs, his aquatints, artwork copies. There is even a small piano keyboard near the entrance. The silence is broken only by occasional squirrel's tip-tap sequence on the roof. Dudok de Wit is confidently seated by his animator's desk, concentrated, serene and with that particular, curious gaze that certain serious children have. Here is the collection of his thoughts on animation, life and utter happiness.

ANIMATING COMMERCIALS

How artistic or how commercial should an animated project be? It depends on the project. For instance, when I was making TV commercials earlier in my career, each film was clearly aimed at a large and varied audience. While a commercial can have originality and even a distinct artistic look, the main priority is always its sales message, not its artistic strength. The film only exists because it must sell a product. To me, a commercial can be an example of extraordinary skill, but it cannot really be called art.

The basic story ideas for my commercials were always written by the advertising agencies, and those agencies also had the final say on the originality of each project or the lack of originality. I accepted those conditions because I enjoyed commercials. Most of them were quite innovative, with an understated commercial message, and I felt that I was learning a lot from them. I could, for instance, explore elements such as the eloquence of the film language, the emotionality of the movements and the graphic qualities of light and shadows.

ANIMATING SHORT FILMS

Short films remind me of poems; they tend to celebrate creativity and individuality. The filmmakers usually write the stories themselves, and they have full artistic control. They have the freedom to choose the kind of effect the film should have on the spectators. For instance, the film does not necessarily have to please. It's true that to be eligible for funding, each film must pass through a selection process by the funding organisations, but many of those organisations are quite supportive of non-commercial, artistic films.

ANIMATING A FEATURE FILM

An animated feature can contain strong artistic qualities, yet it is also a commercial product, since the investors usually hope to see a profit or at least a return of their investments. The filmmaker understands this commercial side, and crucially, he or she also understands that the film must attract the full attention of the audience for the whole duration.

There are investors who are willing to back an animated art house movie, but not many, since it's a high-risk investment for them, even if the film receives critical acclaim when it is released. *The Red Turtle* is an art house film or "film d'auteur". The producers in Japan and France were clear on that, and they were aware of the financial risk. During the development and production stages, I listened a lot to feedback from my producers and my collaborators, but I also kept a strong loyalty to my artistic vision. On top of that, I saw it as my challenge and my privilege to integrate as much as I could the artistic visions of my most creative collaborators.

Some of the producers applied pressure on me to aim for a wider audience. Like me, they wanted the film to stand out for its artistic strength, yet they were also a bit nervous about the film becoming too arty and therefore too difficult to distribute. Sometimes we agreed, sometimes we didn't, but on the whole, I was very lucky with them. Most of the time, they had good suggestions, and right from the start, they were amazingly respectful of my choices.

The Red Turtle had many moments of serenity and of slow storytelling. Without those moments of fine quality, I would not have considered making the film. But this choice made the film fragile during the development and production phases, and the producers, understandably, often questioned me on this.

ANIMATION SKILLS

In everyday language, we talk about the skill of an animator, but to be precise, animators need to develop a combination of skills. I'm referring here to animators who use the classic hand-drawn-animation technique. We need to draw well, we need to understand movement and we need to be good actors. Another skill is less often discussed, even though it has a huge value: the skill to animate with good taste, charm and charisma. For instance, we can animate a character with elegant movements and well-defined emotions, but the character can be totally charmless, unappealing even. I often see that in animated films, including my own work. Charm is hard to define verbally and charisma is even harder. I have asked many friends and colleagues what they can say about the magnetic effect of charismatic individuals, and relatively few had lucid answers. We often want our animated characters to be charismatic, and the best way to discuss this with colleagues is to look at examples.

Some animators are simply never strong on charm and charisma, and they should ideally concentrate on the scenes where charm and charisma are not a priority. An alternative solution, sensitive but effective, is to pass their animation, after they have completed it, on to another animator who is able to retouch the most charmless details.

Animators, like actors, have individual styles and personalities that influence their work consciously and subconsciously.

When we begin a new production and we start looking for freelance animators, each animator should, in an ideal world, be carefully selected by the equivalent of a casting agent. For instance, some animators are good at complex, organic movements, while others are better at simple, stylish movements; some animators are good at loud and generous acting, while others are better at delicate acting and so on. When I direct a film, I become very sensitive to the skills, the styles and the personalities of the individual animators. The same applies to the background artists and, depending on the project, to all other creative members of the team. The quality of understanding between us is really precious.

I'm a skilled animator, not a master animator. I have worked with master animators, and their animation talents are glorious. For me, the important thing is that my main skills, such as animation, direction, drawing and storytelling, have so far been in tune with each other. I couldn't have wished for more.

ARIELLE BASSET

My wife Arielle knew from the very beginning that I would give a lot of my time to my career. I usually worked sixty to seventy hours per week, also during the period when we were a family. Despite that, she accepted that we would be together. For some partners, it would be unacceptable, I imagine. I deeply admire her understanding.

She has a respectful and positive attitude towards my creativity and I need that; otherwise we would have had a very difficult relationship. I owe her a lot. I have often asked for her opinion, for instance, on my storyboards, which she gave with honesty. She said simply what she felt, not giving compliments for compliments' sake: just concise, sincere feedback. Even when she hesitated or when she had nothing to say, I considered that as useful information.

Unlike me, Arielle is very knowledgeable in classical cultures. When we were in our twenties, she would open my eyes to the paintings by Vermeer, for instance, and explain how she was attracted to their stillness and timelessness. Her love for art was contagious; it opened my perception, and once that opened, it didn't close anymore. She educated me in classical architecture and took me to Florence, amongst other places. She introduced me to great singers such as Maria Farantouri and Amália Rodrigues.

ARTIST

It has always been a clear fact for me that I'm not a pure artist. I see an artist as someone who explores the deepest self, the subtle realms, mostly for the joy of exploration or to respond to a deep longing. An artist tries to find something that feels truly original. When I'm making a film, part of me is an artist, but other parts of me are also a craftsman, a storyteller and an entertainer. And all of me is an eternal student, like so many of my colleagues are. We learn new rules, we make our own rules and we happily break them.

ARTISTIC FILM

It's hard to say precisely when a film is artistic or not, since a film is not a single creative expression but a combination of creative expressions. For instance, the main expressions are usually the story, the design, the acting, the film language and the music. Some of these expressions can be extremely artistic, while others within the same film can be classical or even commercial.

BLUES MUSIC

Blues music is not suitable for animation, as far as I know. There is something raw in the blues that disappears when you carefully work on an animated film. Even if the animation itself is raw and gutsy, the typical energy of blues music is compromised. Blues is about improvisation, it belongs to the moment, and animation is not compatible with that kind of improvisation. I have never seen the essence of the blues in animation, and though I often play the blues myself, I have not felt a desire to bring the two together.

CLASSICAL MUSIC

Many animators and a lot of editors have a passion for music, which makes total sense since film language and musical language have so much in common, the way we work with technique, timing and feeling. Regarding my decision to have a composition by Leoš Janáček in the string quartet sequence of *The Red Turtle*, the choice was obvious. In that sequence, the main character is hallucinating, and the music had to stand apart from the score. It had to be quirky, bizarre and at the same time attractive. I discovered Janáček on the radio, and I felt that his style would be appropriate, with his chamber music from the twentieth century, while the musicians in the film would be dressed in costumes from the Mozart era. Since I didn't have time to study Janáček more, I asked my assistant editor, a professional musician, to help me. He preselected a dozen compositions, and I chose this amazing section from *Intimate Pages*. The composition is not round and soft – I would call it zigzagged.

Three of my short films were inspired by classical music. Only when I had an idea of the main melody, the choice of instruments and the composition's main emotions, could I start with the visual development of each film. With those films, the music was my muse. In contrast and to my surprise, I didn't know what I wanted for *The Red Turtle*, and I had almost no suggestions to give to the composer, Laurent Perez del Mar. I explained to him that I had a preference for the impressionists like Debussy, for the inclusion of a cello and that I imagined a three-beat rhythm, but that was all, and I simply couldn't come up with an indication for the musical theme. Laurent proposed his own ideas, of course, full of poetry and emotion, and I was delighted with them. His music was sometimes descriptive, and at other times, he would introduce emotions that were different from the visually expressed emotions. The film has no dialogue, and it was important to respect the many quiet, atmospheric scenes, with the sound of the breeze in the forest, for instance, or the gentle lapping of the waves on the beach. Laurent understood this well, and his score blended seamlessly with those quiet moments.

CLICHÉ

Can a film use clichés and still be artistic? I think so, as long as they are not used excessively. Besides, film language, like verbal language, uses established codes, and the difference between a film language code and a cliché is not always clear. I believe a cliché can be applied with style and flair. Meanwhile, between the clichés or alongside the clichés, the film can be artistically fulfilling for the makers and for the spectators.

Do we imitate work created by other people? Of course we do. We take clues from other artists that we very much admire, we pay homage to them, we emulate their styles and we copy their ideas. I have been inspired by Western European comics' artists and short filmmakers from Central Europe and Russia, amongst others. However, just straightforward imitation without any inventiveness is no fun. It may be helpful to improve our technical skills, and there may be other reasons, but ultimately it is much less fulfilling than being creative. We may imitate or emulate other creative work, but when we make it our own, when we try to give it new meaning, for instance, we immediately begin to feel the fine excitement of creativity.

CREATIVE PROCESS – THE UNKNOWN

One of the biggest attractions of a creative profession is the exploration of the unknown. Exploring the unknown may sound a bit dramatic, since all we seem to be doing is working with our imagination, but when we are fully on a project, the exploration can be intense and all-consuming, and it can even be quite profound. When I'm in a storyboard phase, for instance, I think of ideas night and day, during moments of insomnia, while doing physical activities and even during concerts. While I'm in this phase, I have difficulties reading books and watching films that are not subject-related, and I become hyper aware of symbols and metaphors everywhere around me. Exploration is not only a matter of finding good ideas, but it is also about experimenting with the rich chemistry between those ideas. The storyboard phase can last for several months with short films, and with my last feature length film, it lasted for about four years.

Exploring the unknown can be a very attractive activity, but it is only step one. Step two is making the unknown known and presentable to other people. This is a bigger adventure, and it is risky, because we all know too well that we may fail, however much time we invest in it.

CREATIVE PROCESS – IMAGES

How do I get images and ideas? Visual images induced by hallucinogens and by mind-altering experiences have never inspired my creative work. Neither have I used images or ideas from my nighttime dreams so far. Daydreaming is my trusted method for getting inspiration, and two different ways for receiving images stand out. The first way is to ask myself questions about the kind of images I want to create, and I let my imagination come up with visual answers. This is comparable to doing research, but I'm researching my imagination only.

The second way is simply being receptive to the sudden unexpected appearance of an image into my consciousness. It arrives seemingly out of nowhere, and it can appear anytime, anywhere and usually when I am alone. This probably happens to everybody, I guess, but in my case, I'm very alert for these sudden images, and I welcome them. When an image appears, I examine it straight away, and I decide if it can be used. Sometimes it has a narrative quality; it tells part of a story. If the image is interesting, it will generate a rush of pleasure, similar to the pleasure of receiving a sudden, clear insight.

As I said, it seems to appear out of nowhere, though I find the concept of the unconscious extremely useful, and I believe the image actually comes out of the unconscious, most likely the collective unconscious. If the image chooses to appear suddenly in my consciousness, this can well be because I was searching for it. In that case, it appears after an incubation period that may have lasted hours, days or even years. The longest period so far in my experience has been thirty-six years. In this instance, I had an idea for a story, an unusual and atmospheric story, but some crucial elements were missing. The story didn't flow well. Keeping the work-in-progress story tucked away somewhere in my memory, in the incubation area of my memory, if there is such a thing, I would look at it with regular intervals to see if anything had evolved. One important element revealed itself recently, after a thirty-six year long waiting period, and that was a great moment.

There is a third, external way of obtaining images and ideas, and I use it in combination with the first two ways: doing research. I look at images from any source, read books, talk with people, go on location and I explore my own personal experiences. The research is nourished by a passionate curiosity, a curiosity that continues even after the film is completed.

CREATIVE PROCESS

Our access to the creative process can be painfully fragile. I'm talking here about drawing and filmmaking, in other words about creativity with a physical end result in mind. There are several obvious methods to improve our access to the creative process, to prepare the ground for it, and I usually talk about these methods when I teach.

Ultimately, we don't own creativity – nobody does. We don't own our creative ideas, our art or our originality. This has always been obvious to me. Meanwhile, on an everyday practical level, we talk about his creativity, her art, my art etc. We make it personal, and on that level, we take certain responsibilities for the work we do. But ultimately, we can't claim ownership.

Does it actually matter? I don't think it does while we are creative; we do what we do. But when we work with other people, the understanding that we don't personally own creativity does a lot of good to our attitude. It relaxes the ego, and it reduces ego competition. Ego competition has its own unique way of motivating people of course, but my most respectful, most enjoyable and most efficient collaborations have always been relatively free of that kind of competition.

DANCE

As a young adult, I discovered experimental, contemporary dance, especially dance performances from East Asia, and that is now one of my biggest passions, one that I share with Arielle. We often attend performances in London, and I sit there, watching in a state of utter bliss.

Though I consider contemporary dance a huge inspiration for my creativity, I have never been tempted to animate dancers. It just wouldn't feel right. I have seen films where dancers were animated by animators who clearly have a passion for dance movements, and each time, I thought: the animation may be good, but you have missed the point. Dancers challenge the limitations of the human body and the limits of the stage, and when they succeed in doing this in an original way, the result is simply magical. But in animation, those limitations are almost entirely taken away; those parameters are dropped. An animated dance performance can still be wonderfully entertaining, but I'm referring to the essence of dance, where the dancers express themselves with movements and emotions that resonate with our own deepest emotions. These performances can have a lasting effect on us. On the other hand, when an animator, instead of animating dancing characters, wishes to translate the essence of a dance performance into an abstract piece of animation with stylised shapes and stylised movements, the result can be fascinating. Otherwise, like with the blues and with rock and folk music, some things just lose too much when they are recreated in animation.

DOWNSIDE OF VISUAL STORYTELLING

Another example of a limitation of animation is a disadvantage of visual storytelling. People sometimes assume that all stories can be told in animation and in a way that is true, at least superficially. However, some stories exist to be told in the written form only or orally. That's when they are powerful. I'm thinking for example of a mythological story belonging to a society with a strong tradition for oral storytelling. These stories invite the readers or listeners to use their own visual imagination.

A film goes against this; it uses the filmmaker's visual imagination, not that of a spectator. That's what the spectator expects from a film, and there are very appropriate stories for this medium.

FEEDBACK

When we create a film, especially when we work alone on a short film, I strongly feel that we need feedback along the way, even if it is only once or twice. We need to verify the effect of our creation on individual people. They may see things that we don't see, and we need to hear that. I rely on feedback from my spouse, as I said before, from my collaborators and occasionally from a friend outside the animation industry. Professional feedback can be excellent; however, a reaction from a well-chosen non-professional, a child even, can be very useful too.

But at the same time, I surrender to my deepest self, I listen to it and I don't let anyone influence this process. Therefore, paradoxically, I listen exclusively to my deepest self, yet I also listen to feedback from people. The dynamic between these two approaches is not fixed, it's alive and I tend to evaluate it all the time. How do I evaluate it? I don't really know – I just keep looking at the two priorities, and somehow the right balance becomes obvious.

HAKUIN EKAKU (1686–1769)

Around 1981, the Royal Academy in London hosted an exhibition called *The Great Japan Exhibition*, and I discovered there a book called *Zenga and Nanga, Paintings by Japanese Monks and Scholars*. Seeing the ink paintings and calligraphy of the Zen priest Hakuin Ekaku, my creativity suddenly became focussed. It was the first time in my life that I could so totally identify with an art form, and it happened to be an art form from a culture far away, from the other side of the planet. In the same book, I also discovered the ink paintings by Sengai Gibon and Nantembo Nakahara. I recognised myself in the way these artists were sensitive to composition, to space, to elegance, to spontaneity and to simplicity.

I will never imitate this art; it is not my skill, and I haven't grown up in that culture. But the essence of these ink paintings was the biggest inspiration for me. Without discovering Zen art, I could never have made *The Red Turtle*, for instance.

INTUITION

I remember that brief video interview from three years ago where I talked about my rational side and my intuitive side. I sighed when I found it on the Internet, because what I said in that interview was not right. I talked about my rational side and my intuition, when in truth I meant reason in general and especially intuition in general. I deeply believe that while our access to intuition may have a unique, personal flavour, intuition itself is beyond the personal. It's vast and exquisite, and to me, it is the transition between the unconscious and consciousness.

LONGING

When I was in my late twenties, I suddenly realised that I was going through life with a permanent, quiet feeling of deep longing. The object of this longing was not clear; all I could see was that the object was subtle and not specific, that somehow it was beyond everything. Meanwhile, the longing itself was unmistakable. For instance, my longing was made conscious over and over again by music, especially by music in the minor key. It was made conscious by moments of melancholia, by moments of loneliness but also by happy moments, lying in the grass and looking at the treetops. Deep longing is a form of suffering, but I trusted it, and I found it extremely pure and beautiful.

After that recognition, my life's purpose became finer; I changed from being a confused seeker of general happiness to a serious seeker of the ultimate, whatever it is. I also began to see this longing in the behaviour of many individuals, even when they were not aware of it. They would, for instance, translate it into idealism; they would long for the good old days, for the perfect partner, for fame, for status etc. But the yearning I felt was deeper than a desire for fame or a nostalgia for an idyllic past. That's how I conceived my short film *Father and Daughter* many years later. I acknowledged the beauty of spiritual longing, and I symbolised it in the longing of a daughter for her absent father.

MOVEMENTS

In animation, we have different kinds of movements: the movement of each character, the choreography between them, the movement of the story, graphic movements, camera movements, the movements of the edit and of course the music. The joy of a filmmaker is to play with all these movements individually and to play with the relationship between them.

NATURE

A couple of people have asked me how much I identified with the main character of *The Red Turtle*. I certainly identified with him, even though I would have behaved differently if I had been in his situation, stranded on a desert island. I also identified with the woman in the story and with their son. Furthermore, I felt a strong identification with the marine turtle, the forest, the island, the clouds and very much with the horizon, with the space around the human characters, especially around their heads, and all other spaces, like the air just above the meadow. I believe it is natural for a visual storyteller to feel a strong empathy with every character and every element. This empathy is so evident that I almost take it for granted, and I see it as an expression of animism.

I used to think that animism had to do with superstition. Growing up half a century ago in a rational Western society that strongly believed in the difference between creatures that are alive and material objects that are lifeless, there was no room for individuals like me who somehow sensed that everything is alive through and through. But the animist perspective never really left me, and part of me is a modern animist. My respect for nature is huge and unconditional, and the story of *The Red Turtle* celebrates that. It celebrates that we are nature, that we always have been nature and that we always will be. With nature, I mean all nature of course, not just the vegetation and the creatures, but also the cycle of life and death, the violent side of nature and all the natural phenomena.

NIGHT

The night is a good place. Inside the house or outside, lit by the moon or by the stars only, I feel safe in the night, especially outside in nature. Some locations may hide danger, but there are safe locations too, and once we realise that the night is also on our side, we don't need a flashlight. A flashlight is aggressive; it pushes the night away. Without artificial light, the night becomes fascinating, physically and symbolically. It reveals our unconscious, though we can't see what is in it, but we can, but we can't, yet we can … and we can explore this mystery if we choose to go there. Deep in the night, we slow down, and our vision becomes peripheral; we have an extraordinary alertness, and we notice more than we realise.

PERFECTIONISM

The drive towards perfection comes with our animation profession. It's good for our work, very good in fact, and it's not so good for our health. Perfectionism is hard and pitiless, and it can carelessly drive us to exhaustion. I have learned over time that while we value perfectionism, we should value self-compassion at the same time.

One of our greatest assets is our capacity to judge our work. We judge whether it is good enough, whether we should continue improving it or whether we should wait and sleep over it. Basically, we have two very distinct ways of judging, of making a decision. The first one is our focussed way, choosing between yes and no, for instance, or between good and bad. It's binary. It tends to be analytical, sharp and confident, and it's efficient but not necessarily always wise. With the second way, we are more open; we look at all aspects and at the way the different aspects interact with each other. This way uses fewer preconceptions. It is more complex, and as a result, we are more hesitant and more prone to defer the decision-making. Even so, we favour it when we are creative, especially when we are in the development phases of a project. In my experience, the open way of judging also increases my receptivity to chance, luck and serendipity.

Both ways of decision-making are essential, the focussed way and the wider picture way, and if we neglect the focussed way, we will suffer from too much hesitation. I had a habit of neglecting the focussed way during my career, and I know I'm not unique. This neglect slowed me down too much. The solution was to trust the focussed way more and to practice it.

Regarding hesitation, whenever I can't make up my mind and I'm stuck in hesitation, and when the focussed way of thinking is not appropriate in that case, I choose between two classic solutions: I leave that decision aside, if I can, and forget about it for a while to come back to it later, or I ask someone for a second opinion.

RICHARD PURDUM PRODUCTIONS

In 1980, I arrived at Richard Purdum's studio just after its opening, and I worked there for about twelve years on and off as a freelancer, initially as Dick's animation assistant and gradually as an animator and an animation director. We were small teams making quality commercials. Dick Purdum, now retired, is extremely discreet about his talent, yet I see him as one of the rare master animators alive today. In my eyes, he was clearly my teacher, and I was one of his apprentices – I told him this recently, and he just laughed. He wouldn't teach me, that was not his style, but he would encourage me to discover things by experimentation, and I also learned from him by osmosis, by observing him. I learned from both him and Jill Thomas, his wife and producer, how to work with each collaborator individually, how to be a realistic perfectionist and basically how to be a professional. I deeply respect them, and I still often think of the things I have learned from them.

SHADOWS

If I have a visual style, I would describe it as the use of light and shadows. When I see a play of light through a row of trees, for instance, and the shadows on the ground shape the landscape so gracefully, I just have to act on that. I want to explore that and play with that. But shadows have an unusual, abstract quality; they are not characters, and it is understandable why many animators are not interested in them.

I choose to include shadows in my films for a combination of reasons. Shadows that are related to sunlight can communicate the time of the day. In other words, they can create a unique ambiance. Secondly, shadows are striking, dark shapes. Their graphic quality is part of the overall composition. For me, each of these two reasons is already strong enough to choose the use of light and shadows. Shadows can also accentuate the relationship between the character and the background; they bond the two together. The shapes and edges of the shadows can reveal the shapes and the textures of the surfaces. In other words, we can use shadows to sculpt shapes. And finally, when a moving character casts a shadow on the ground, the shadow always moves in perfect synchronisation with the character. Spectators naturally enjoy watching synchronisation. Even when they don't focus their attention on the actual shadows, they feel their presence.

I realise that these qualities are subtle and that many subtle qualities are enjoyed on a subconscious level, not even consciously. But the point is that they are enjoyed, and these qualities add up, and they bring a film to life.

SENSITIVITY

I occasionally give masterclasses at art schools and universities, and the content invariably touches on the elusive subjects such as creativity, intuition and the narrative flow. If a member of the audience only retains one word from the class, and forgets about all other words, I hope it is the word "sensitivity". Everything I endeavour to pass on is summarised in that single word. To me, sensitivity is the gateway towards a greater creativity. If we are deeply interested in sensitivity, and especially in an ever-growing sensitivity, the quality of our creativity will improve.

SPIRITUALITY

Spirituality can be associated with religion, but it does not have to be. I see spirituality simply as a person's passion for the most profound aspects of life. At the same time, I recognise spirituality as a deep longing for total happiness or total love or for the absolute. Actually, it is a longing for something that can't really be named, because it is too fine, too all-inclusive and too extraordinary to be described in any language. I have tried many times to put it into words, out of curiosity, and I have not succeeded. But we can be aware of it, or we can at least have intimations of it. As a concession here, I'll call it deep happiness.

This deep happiness is most intimate and at the same time utterly selfless. Once we begin to sense that this happiness is real and not some kind of fantasy, we long for it and search for a way to move closer to it. That movement is spirituality, in my opinion. That movement, by the way, also stimulates our passion for the finest qualities of life, such as trust, compassion, our connectedness with nature, honesty, clarity, wisdom and of course love, to name but a few.

The movement towards this deep happiness may be really simple, when we look back, but when we are in the middle of it, it is unlike anything else and full of paradoxes. It can even drive us to despair until we reach a turning point, if we are lucky, after which we simply surrender and trust our intuition.

When the time comes that we fully realise the deep happiness and we understand that it is always present, we just want to abide in it, totally and unconditionally. It is the most natural thing to do. On the surface, we continue experiencing life's ups and downs, and we may respond to them or not, but at the same time we know this quiet happiness. We know that we are home. Spirituality has then acquired a new meaning, where the longing and the seeking have stopped and the grateful exploration of life has begun.

This is my angle on spirituality, based on my experience. I hope that I don't sound too abstract, and if I do, I apologise. I find the subject of spirituality extraordinarily attractive, but due to its subtle and subjective nature, it is hard to talk about it. Hopefully it makes sense why I see a connection between creativity and spirituality. Creativity can give us so much. It can be wonderfully emotional, it can comfort us or shock us out of our preconceptions, it can create bonds between us, it can stimulate us on an intellectual level. But ultimately, when I'm creative and when I appreciate creativity from other people, I find it tremendously inspiring when I see that there is no separation between creativity and spirituality.

On a practical level, how can I create a film that may point towards this unnameable, this deep happiness? My priority is to be aware of this fine bliss. As I just said, I simply abide in it. And meanwhile, if this bliss has an influence on the quality of my work, it is my task to recognise that influence and to nurture that. When I recognise it in my work, it manifests itself typically as simplicity or as beauty.

Could this simplicity or beauty, if it is present in my work, make a spectator aware of deep happiness? Maybe just for a moment or maybe not at all, but I have no influence on this.

TAKAHATA ISAO

Takahata was not an animator; he couldn't draw, but he had the sensitivity of an animation director, and I wanted to explore this as much as possible with him and learn from his experience.

He was very cultured, he was fascinated by symbols, he was fascinated by conscious and subconscious messages, but there was more. He directed a film that includes haikus, *My Neighbours the Yamadas*. We can't make films like that. No one can; it's impossible. Haikus are too pristine, too quiet to translate into films, yet he did it, and I'm in awe of that. I had the privilege to have long conversations with him about the story of *The Red Turtle*. Though our conversations were slow, because we always spoke through an interpreter, that suited me very well, and it also taught me to be more precise. We were both very discreet about our personal lives; however, our conversations about the project's subtle qualities created an intimate ambiance. I was extremely fond of him.

Appendix 2

Michael Dudok de Wit's List of Inspiring Films

M ICHAEL DUDOK DE WIT has written down a list of films, both live-action and animation, that he finds inspiring. He enriched his list with several "treasures, made by women and about women", pointing out at the same time that he's been inspired "by relatively many films made by female directors". According to Dudok de Wit, "the list should ideally be ten or twenty times longer, but fourteen is already a lot".[1]

1. *The Immigrant* by Charlie Chaplin (1917, USA, live-action, 30 mins). I can't create a list of inspiring films without immediately thinking of Chaplin's humanity and charisma.

2. *The Heron and the Crane* by Yuri Norstein (1974, USSR, 10 mins). This short film was my introduction to visual poetry, and I still see it as one of the most beautiful films ever made in the history of animation.

3. *The Enigma of Kaspar Hauser* by Werner Herzog (1974, Germany, live-action, 109 mins). I'm deeply touched by the

innocence and strange wisdom of this highly unusual man, Kaspar Hauser, played by the eccentric Bruno Schleinstein. Based on a true story, Hauser was a foundling who at the age of 17 could hardly speak.

4. *Dersu Uzala* by Akira Kurosawa (1975, Japan, live-action, 142 mins). Especially the sequence after about 45 minutes, when Captain Arsenyev and Dersu Uzala are lost and have to find a way to survive a storm. This film is a fine example of friendship between men and of our profound respect for nature.

5. *Why Me?* by Janet Perlman (1978, Canada, 10 mins). A gem. A doctor breaks the news to his patient that he only has five minutes left to live.

6. *The Man Who Planted Trees* by Frédéric Back (1987, Canada, 30 mins). This deeply moving story, especially the story's ending, with the old shepherd standing under the large tree, fills me with awe. I also chose this film for Frédéric Back's graceful animation and the hauntingly beautiful score by Normand Roger.

7. *The Black Dog* by Alison De Vere (1987, United Kingdom, 18 mins). A rare example of a short film about a spiritual journey. Alison De Vere, with her trust in her personal journey and with her vulnerability, encouraged me to live my journey and to value my vulnerability.

8. *My Neighbour Totoro* by Hayao Miyazaki (1988, Japan, 86 mins). Two young sisters are waiting at a bus stop for the arrival of their father: what a magical, iconic moment in the history of animation. I believe that Miyazaki, more than any other filmmaker, has a natural understanding of animism.

9. *Creature Comforts* by Nick Park (1989, United Kingdom, 5 mins). I'm referring to the very first episode, before

Creature Comforts was made into a series. A collection of brilliantly animated interviews. The voices are not from voice actors but from everyday people.

10. *Two Sisters* (*Entre deux soeurs*) by Caroline Leaf (1991, Canada, 10 mins). A beautiful, emotional character study. I also selected this film for Caroline Leaf's stylised animation and for her understanding of light.

11. *Revolver* (*Här är Karusellen*) by Jonas Odell, Stig Berquist, Martti Ekstrand and Lars Ohlson (1994, Sweden, 8 mins). A drowning man has flashbacks. I have watched this film over and over again for its extraordinary, nightmarish originality.

12. *My Neighbours the Yamadas* by Isao Takahata (1999, Japan, 104 mins). This film contains some of the finest haiku sensitivity that I'm aware of, for instance, when the father is noticing the first falling snowflakes. Takahata also demonstrates a deep respect for human nature, with all its flaws.

13. *Peripheria* by David Coquard-Dassault (2015, France, 12 mins). Again, pure visual poetry. I have chosen this short for its striking beauty and its unique ambiance created by abandoned tower blocks and roaming dogs.

14. *This Magnificent Cake!* by Emma De Swaef and Marc James Roels (2018, Belgium, 44 mins). Rarely have I seen such an exquisite, disturbing sense of humour, and meanwhile this film manages to be gently touching. A compilation of highly original stories set in Belgium's colonial Africa.

18 December 2019.

NOTE

1. Michael Dudok de Wit's email to Andrijana Ružić, 18 December 2019.

Appendix 3

Proust Questionnaire by Michael Dudok de Wit for Andrijana Ružić (14 August 2017)

1. What is your idea of perfect happiness?
Feeling deep gratitude. To me this is true happiness.

2. What is your greatest fear?
Observing the continuation of our excessive wasting and our polluting. It's not so much my greatest fear but my greatest sadness.

3. What is the trait you most deplore in yourself?
I deplore the moments when I'm not listening to people.

4. What is the trait you most deplore in others?
The same.

5. Which living person do you most admire?
The respectful person.

6. What is your greatest extravagance?
Eating.

7. What is your current state of mind?
Generally healthy, I hope.

8. What do you consider the most overrated virtue?
Honesty. Superficial honesty is overrated because it is compromised by our emotions and our conscious and unconscious beliefs. On the other hand, profound honesty, coming from a quiet part of ourselves, is an underrated virtue. Or rather, its existence is not recognised enough.

9. On what occasion do you lie?
I lie to myself and, as a result, to others when I'm not really listening to myself.

10. What do you most dislike about your appearance?
I prefer to skip this question.

11. Which living person do you most despise?
I don't despise people, but I despise certain things that people do. Causing suffering, any suffering, to people and to animals, is the worst thing we can do.

12. What is the quality you most like in a man?
Wisdom. I'm not referring to the wisdom that we can study in books; that's more about acquiring knowledge and not necessarily about being wise. I'm referring to the simple, intuitive wisdom that men and women have and children too in their own way – the wisdom that manifests itself naturally in our daily lives.

13. What is the quality you most like in a woman?
Wisdom.

14. Which words or phrases do you most overuse?
"Um", the sound expressing a hesitation and used as a filler when I talk.

15. What or who is the greatest love of your life?
Life itself.

16. When and where were you happiest?
The first evening with the woman who is now my wife. We were both students in the city of Geneva and on a warm spring evening we went for a walk along the shore of the lake. We didn't yet realise how much we loved each other.

17. Which talent would you most like to have?
The talent of making people laugh warmly.

18. If you could change one thing about yourself, what would it be?
My memory is fine, and when it is not, I take notes. But an excellent memory would be wonderful.

19. What do you consider your greatest achievement?
So far: learning what I've needed to learn and unlearning what I've needed to unlearn.

20. If you were to die and come back as a person or a thing, what would it be?
A boy or a girl growing up in a loving community.

21. Where would you most like to live?
Actually, where I live now, in a street with a nice ambience on a hill in London.

22. What is your most treasured possession?
Good health. It's not really a possession, of course. It is something to nurture.

23. What do you regard as the lowest depth of misery?
Feeling unworthy to continue living. That must be an extreme form of misery.

24. What is your favourite occupation?

Two occupations: simply feeling deep gratitude, as I mentioned before, and deep dreamless sleep. Strictly speaking, both are non-occupations.

25. What is your most marked characteristic?

I would like to think it is sensitivity, especially sensitivity to ambiances and moods. I experienced painful oversensitivity for many years, but I gradually saw sensitivity as a great blessing. It's a very fine way of appreciating every moment for its uniqueness.

26. What do you most value in your friends?

Closeness.

27. Who are your favourite writers?

Regarding writers of fiction, I don't have favourite writers, but I have favourite stories, such as Jack London's *Koolau the Leper* and Jean Giono's *The Man Who Planted Trees*, *The Old Man and the Sea* by Ernest Hemmingway, *Deogratias* by Jean-Philippe Stassen, *Tintin in Tibet* by Hergé and his studio, *Moominland Midwinter* by Tove Jansson and *The Song of Wandering Aengus*, an exquisite poem by W.B. Yeats. I have read these stories at least twice and some of them at least a dozen times.

28. Who is your hero of fiction?

Jiro Taniguchi wrote the graphic novel *The Walking Man*. The protagonist is an ordinary man, walking through the suburban streets of a Japanese city and simply observing life around him. It's a remarkable book where the hero is a normal guy.

Another fictitious character I love is Winnie the Pooh; I mean the original character from the books by A.A. Milne, illustrated by E.H. Shepard.

And thirdly, Charlie Chaplin's charismatic character of the tramp.

29. Which historical figure do you most identify with?

There isn't any historical figure, but lately my thoughts go to our prehistoric ancestors, the hunter-gatherers, because they must have had an extraordinary attunement to nature. I don't idealise them – they most likely had their share of suffering – but their relationship with nature must have been more total and more complete than we will ever experience. My empathy towards them woke up when I visited caves where they used to live in the South of France.

30. Who are your heroes in real life?

People who are deeply respectful, to others and to themselves.

31. What are your favourite names?

I find Italian names and Sanskrit names strikingly elegant.

32. What is it that you most dislike?

Two things: strong physical pain and extreme numbness.

33. What is your greatest regret?

I regret not doing something alone with my father, just the two of us, like going for a long walk, during the last years preceding his death.

34. How would you like to die?

Consciously.

35. What is your motto?

"Yes".

Appendix 4

Collaborators, Other Filmmakers and Film Critics about Michael Dudok de Wit and His Films

ONE OF THE MOST interesting parts of my book research consisted in contacting Dudok de Wit's collaborators. I would usually send them a list of questions regarding their contribution to his films: about the most challenging tasks they affronted, about their expectations and finally their gratifications. I would ask them also to share some anecdotes from that time or only their own observations regarding his personality. And to my surprise, all contacted persons responded me with their recollections that have immensely enriched the content of this book. I have also contacted a number of other animation directors who shared with me their observations about their favourite Dudok de Wit's films. The small number of excerpts from the articles of several influential film critics and animation historians conclude this atypical appendix on critical reception of Dudok de Wit's body of work.

MIKHAIL ALDASHIN,[1] DIRECTOR AND ANIMATOR

My father used to play button accordion. And he was often away on business trips. I would wait for him. And I would miss him. Every time I see Michael's film *Father and Daughter*, I think of my father, and I cannot hold back my tears. I think that whoever sees Michael's film remembers their father and maybe how they waited for them in their childhood. A beautiful film indeed.

GIANNALBERTO BENDAZZI,[2] ANIMATION HISTORIAN

Father and Daughter is a one-of-a-kind work, like a poem or a painting. In its own way, it was the ultimate auteur film, the epitome of a genre. It doesn't try to please the audience; it conveys a special feeling and a special appearance which the audience is free to accept or not. It doesn't mind entertaining, and it also has some serious message. It is written, designed, animated and directed by one person, whose inspiration can't be misrepresented or modified by too many collaborators.

SERGE BESSET,[3] COMPOSER, *THE MONK AND THE FISH*

Michael is the best! When he was working on *The Monk and the Fish*, the walls on his apartment were covered with pieces of paper with the numbers and descriptions of the music, meticulously studied frame by frame. At that time, the numeric did not exist, and the music was being transferred on a 35 mm film…

MARCO BELLANO,[4] ANIMATION HISTORIAN

Among Michael Dudok De Wit's films, *The Monk and the Fish* stands out because of how the idea of variation is delightfully ingrained into its poetics. The animation of *The Monk and the Fish* is closely tailored to a piece with this idea: an original set of variations by Serge Besset on *La Folìa*, an ancient and anonymous melody that became popular as a variation material during the late Renaissance and the Baroque. Dudok de Wit's animation complements the musical variations; it is not just a matter of Mickey-Mousing (that is anyway present) but of introducing patterns in the editing, movements, lighting and camera angles that get suddenly disconfirmed by a mutation, with an ironic and satisfying effect on the viewer. This starts to happen even during the opening titles. The French title, *Le Moine et le Poisson*, appears first; the English title follows below but with a twist: it reads just "The Monk and the". The word "Fish" is revealed after an unexpected while! A later short film followed the example of Dudok de Wit and Besset: Hayao Miyazaki's *Pandane to Tamago Hime* (*Mr. Dough and the Egg Princess*, 2010), with variations on *La Folìa* by Joe Hisaishi.

OLGA BOBROWSKA,[5] ANIMATION SCHOLAR, *THE RED TURTLE* REVIEW

In *The Red Turtle*, emotional and sensitive perception overwhelms the intellectual quality of the film: it is as beautiful as banal, and so the creativity is detached from problematic nature of existence. In a sense, it is a hypocrisy since the film promises an extreme focus on an individual being in relation to the world, but in fact it celebrates sentimentality (vide "a punch-line" of the final dance), elaborates ecology in a New Age manner and also reveals certain misogynistic features as the turtle/woman character appears to be inactive and physically dominated by men.

BRUNO BOZZETTO,[6] DIRECTOR AND ANIMATOR

The things that strike me the most in Dudok de Wit's art are the great poetry of his stories, the synthesis, the extraordinary visual images, the sense of emptiness and space, the refined animation and above all an exaggerated attention to details. He knows how to fascinate and excite the spectator with simple gestures of the characters, with a flight of birds or with the rustle of leaves in the tree branches: he reaches the depth of your soul because he simply knows how to use these tiny details. The first time I saw *Father and Daughter*, I was excited and moved as I hadn't been for a long time, and I still remember the old woman's bike that kept falling down or the little girl on the bike returning home faster than usual because the wind blew in her favour ... These apparently insignificant details speak to our heart and make unique this perfect fusion between Oriental artistic refinement and Western visual language: the magnificence and the art of *The Red Turtle* proves it. I believe and insist, however, that the small actions of the characters in his films make Dudok de Wit so great. An important story can be forgotten over time, but what cannot be forgotten is a particular human behaviour.

PAOLA BRISTOT,[7] ARTISTIC DIRECTOR, PICCOLO FESTIVAL ANIMAZIONE

The absolute protagonist of *The Red Turtle* is Nature, and we, the spectators, are the deuteragonists who immerse ourselves in the island step by step. We learn to discover it; to guess the orientations; to know where the pool of fresh water is, where the danger creeps behind the promontory; how great the forest is and where the safest inlet opens; what is the best point for fishing ... because the director presents us with an island that becomes true, with the starry skies in which we recognise the constellations and therefore the position of the cardinal points, in which we understand the time of the day by the quantity of light present and how long it takes to run from one to the other side of the island. The director-demiurge builds a world that becomes a sublime touchstone for us accustomed to an artificial system of life. An heir of the great German Adam Elsheimer and the Nordic European artist travellers, Michael Dudok de Wit also gives us a transfigured reinterpretation of the world, which is not the cherished Arcadia of Claude Lorrain or Poussin, nor a Turner's romantic vision. We are witnessing here a writing degree zero from where we ought to start all over again.

RASTKO ĆIRIĆ,[8] DIRECTOR AND ANIMATOR

At first sight it may seem that the film *Father and Daughter* touched me because I'm a father of two daughters, but it is not the case. It is a film of sophisticated visuals and with a strong emotional point. It is one of four to five films in the history of animation that causes tears and can serve as a crown evidence that animated films are not only comical and not just for children.

OLIVIER COTTE,[9] ANIMATION HISTORIAN

Father and Daughter creates a rare emotional response; the film deals with people, a personal voyage, and is full of moving details filmed with a discernment that shows the filmmaker's sensibility. Without using spectacular techniques or colourful tricks, Michael Dudok de Wit gently invites the viewer to enter the hearts of the characters and their lives. Watching *Father and Daughter* is still a moving experience; the emotion pours forth from the screen and touches you deeply.

PETER DEBRUGE,[10] CHIEF FILM CRITIC, *THE VARIETY, THE RED TURTLE* REVIEW

Washing up on the shores of Cannes after nearly a decade of painstaking under-the-radar toil, Michael Dudok de Wit's hypnotising, entirely dialogue-free *The Red Turtle* is a fable so simple, so pure, it feels as if it has existed for hundreds of years, like a brilliant shard of sea glass rendered smooth and elegant through generations of retelling.

GUY DELISLE,[11] GRAPHIC NOVEL AUTHOR AND CARTOONIST, ASSISTANT ANIMATOR, *THE MONK AND THE FISH*

Michael was such a nice person to work with! His style of animation was very unique for me, I have never worked on something like that. He directly inked certain scenes on the cells! It was the most interesting job I got in my ten years of animation.

BORIVOJ DOVNIKOVIĆ BORDO,[12] DIRECTOR, ANIMATOR AND CARTOONIST

There are a few authors of animated films that can delight a professional animator. This delight happened to me at the first encounter with Michael Dudok de Wit's film *The Monk and the Fish* at the Annecy Festival in 1995. The symbiosis of movement and music, an impeccable stylised animation and an exciting story imbued with a sense of pure joy – this painterly film takes your attention from the first to the last scene and then remains in your life memories forever, like a precious jewel. Later in my life I've seen *The Monk and the Fish* several times in various occasions, and for me, it never lost its perfection.

I am particularly pleased that Michael accomplished all this with a classical cel animation in which the animation mastery comes to the fullest. In addition, the director is a complete author (script, designer, animator) and shares the authorship only with the composer Serge Besset whose rearrangement of *La Folia* becomes an organic part of Michael's animation. This animated film, in the best sense of the term, reminds me somehow of Ravel's "Bolero"!

PAUL DRIESSEN,[13] DIRECTOR, ANIMATOR

What always struck me about Michael's films is the fact that they're not plot driven; the beauty of the design and treatment of his animation and meditative ideas seemed to make the films whole. *The Red Turtle* was very well received for what it was: a moving work of art with subliminal ideas which lifted it above the ordinary structured films. The problem with making features is that it's very difficult for a director to go back to the more personal short form. Although I'm sure Michael will do well with his next animated feature, I'd love to see another short jewel of his hand popping up once in a while.

PIOTR DUMAŁA,[14] DIRECTOR AND ANIMATOR

My favourite Michael's film is *The Monk and the Fish*. I see it as a film about freedom and joy. It is light, beautiful, optimistic, just imagined for animation language, fantastic in its rhythm and synchronisation with music and soft in colours. I like the end of it – open and mysterious.

PASCALE FERRAN,[15] DIRECTOR AND SCREENWRITER, SCRIPT ADAPTATION, *THE RED TURTLE*

I was stunned by the visual beauty of *The Red Turtle*: the extraordinary quality of the animation and all the work that had been done on the soundtrack (sound editing, music, mix), which is of course vital for this film. I think they did an incredible job.

IGOR GRUBIĆ,[16] ARTIST, PRODUCER AND AUTHOR OF DOCUMENTARIES

I have always been magnetically attracted to Dudok de Wit's films: the topics he deals with, his control over the rhythm and the purification of artistic expression tell me that there is a strong spiritual discipline behind an excellent master – someone who is not seduced by the charms of technological hyper-production but who is profoundly dedicated to his work and experiences it deeply. Such an artistic approach is almost identical to the alchemical process, which leaves its mark on both the author himself and the others who come to terms with his work.

PAUL HEATH,[17] FILM CRITIC, *THE HOLLYWOOD NEW, THE RED TURTLE* REVIEW

The Red Turtle is absolutely magnificent. Michael Dudok de Wit has painstakingly spent the best part of a decade making this absolutely stunning animated film, a visual marvel from start to end with stunning animation, delightful story and an emotional punch which you'd expect from the celebrated Studio Ghibli stable.

CLAIRE JENNINGS,[18] FILM PRODUCER, *FATHER AND DAUGHTER*

Michael is a kind and gentle, powerful soul, and my collaboration with him was humbling. He has the touch of a master craftsman which is again manifest in his latest feature *The Red Turtle*. It bears the essential hallmark of lightness that only an animator/director of exceptional talent can deliver. The many pencil lines dance animatedly in harmony with the beautifully chosen subtler levels of sound. The screen echoes the art of true simplicity. To achieve such work, whilst simultaneously directing numerous teams of artists on how to sit within your artistic style and to collaborate with many others regarding story, sound and music, is the mark of a great spirit.

CÉLINE KÉLÉPIKIS,[19] EDITOR, *THE RED TURTLE*

Michael is very close to the human sensibility of *The Red Turtle* being kind and respectful himself. I'm very happy that the long version of his way of telling emotional stories has worked out. When I saw his short films, I kept in mind in what measure the simplicity conveyed emotions, without words ... and finally the challenge was to make it work in a feature film as well.

MARK KERMODE,[20] FILM CRITIC

The Red Turtle is a meditation upon existence, upon loneliness, upon companionship, about birth, death and rebirth. It manages to be all that by combining old cinema, silent cinema and absolutely superb music that blends so beautifully with the sound effects. It is a film with strong elements of fantasy, and yet it is rooted in an island you believe in, in the reality you believe in. Its nighttime sequences almost become monochrome; they are almost taking you back to the origins of cinema. It is a deeply compassionate film and touching and funny and affectionate and insightful, and I was in love with it, I was so swept away with it! Towards the end, the film becomes more profound because it has to do with ageing and so many other things, and I found myself properly crying. It's a work of art; it's a beautiful, beautiful work of art that has genuinely universal appeal. It touches the very essence of what cinema can do and manages to do it by looking back over at the history of cinema, and it makes animation seem more real than what we refer to as real-life action. I encourage everybody to see it because it's just magnificent!

IGOR KOVALYOV,[21] DIRECTOR AND ANIMATOR

Each time I watch *Father and Daughter*, I think: how is it possible to make such an emotional and poetic film by using such a minimum of means? It is minimalist both in terms of image and animation. In one of the scenes, a group of cyclists are going up the hill: the closer they get to the top, the harder it is to pedal, and at a certain point they reach zero speed. It is in this moment that I am preoccupied about whether the characters will be able to reach the top of the hill. But then the director cuts, and we see the same characters calmly riding along a flat road. In that very instant, I start feeling an unexplainable tension, which shortly afterwards turns into a complete relaxation – something that feels like a small orgasm.

JEAN-CHRISTOPHE LIE,[22] CHIEF ANIMATOR ON *THE RED TURTLE*

Michael had drawn a storyboard on paper and produced an animatic. When we started production, we moved on to Cintiq tablets, a technique with which he wasn't yet familiar. Soon he no longer had the time to draw or animate. He was there to guide us and help us to improve the film. There was a constant dialogue between him and the animators. He is probably one of the greatest perfectionists I've met. But he's very open to different viewpoints, and that's very stimulating. We had long and passionate discussions.

JULIEN DE MAN,[23] BACKGROUND SUPERVISOR, *THE RED TURTLE*

Michael is a very respectful and honest person, gentle and humble. He is curious about every aspect of life and happy to live it, like children do sometimes. I remember him being enthusiastic, laughing intensely, walking in socks in the studio, being a bit clumsy, cracking nuts with the doors, chewing his pencils from the mine side, falling asleep for ten seconds during the approval screenings, then suddenly waking up and asking "Can we watch it again please?", thinking that nobody has noticed it ... All of this Michael's moonstruck side, I just love it.

SIMONE MASSI,[24] DIRECTOR, ANIMATOR AND ILLUSTRATOR

I remember Michael Dudok de Wit's figure well. I met him in Zagreb back in 2002. He was talking to Jerzy Kucia and another animator whose name I don't remember. Two things struck me about him: his extreme kindness and the fact that he could not accept the invitation of another festival for economic reasons. He had just won an Oscar with *Father and Daughter*, and he still had financial difficulties! I laughed thinking that for my category, there was no hope whatsoever.

LAURENT PEREZ DEL MAR,[25] COMPOSER, *THE RED TURTLE*

Our collaboration was truly wonderful. Michael gave me an absolute confidence at a very early stage; he was always in an equal mood, very zen, knowing exactly whether it went in the right direction for the movie or not. I find him passionate, extremely gifted and with true human values. I learned a lot from him, both as a director and a friend, but the first thing that comes to mind is that Michael is a very positive person and deeply connected with his emotions. It made me want to try to do the same.

PRIMA LINEA,[26] LINE PRODUCER, *THE RED TURTLE*

Production was launched in July 2013, with a very small team of carefully selected artists. The layout of the scenery began, even though Michael felt the design of the vegetation wasn't yet strong enough and required development, as did the character of the woman. Once more we discovered Michael's perfectionism and how his outlook embraces all aspects of the film, right down to the tiniest details. Each pleat of fabric, each wave of hair: nothing was left to chance.

JILL AND RICHARD PURDUM,[27] FOUNDERS OF RICHARD PURDUM PRODUCTIONS

Michael is not only a creative artist and talented animator; he is also a very gentle and charming person and a terrific team player. As Michael spent more time on his own short films and book illustration, he would come and go from our studio to work on his own projects. We were always very happy to welcome him back when he returned to us to do another commercial. He was always a pleasure to work with and for all of us to have around. Throughout, he remained one of the founding members of our studio family. As you can imagine, we are very proud of him.

BARRY J. C. PURVES,[28] ANIMATOR, DIRECTOR AND SCREENPLAY WRITER

I wish I had the skill of such filmmakers as Michael Dudok De Wit, in whose films, especially my favourite, *The Monk and the Fish* (1994), so much is created with so little. A simple shadow creates a credible geography, and a black line becomes a horizon. The enigmatic story of a monk catching a fish is superficially no more than that, but because the drawings are so simple and everything is about suggestion, the viewer's mind is full of its own meanings. The action progressively takes on a lyrical surreal quality and the ending is simply uplifting. The animation consists of few in-betweens, relying on stunningly synchronised key drawings. The music, based on Corelli, is as much a dramatic part of the film as the animation and design. Everything works together, but it is its deep simplicity that is so powerful. The scene where the monk is jumping in great leaps and bounds sees the animation at its most economical, but also its most evocative and moving.

CHRIS ROBINSON,[29] ARTISTIC DIRECTOR(OTTAWA INTERNATIONAL ANIMATION FESTIVAL), ANIMATION WRITER

Dudok De Wit, Michael: Dutch–British animator. His two Oscar-winning films are *The Monk and the Fish* and *Father and Daughter*. Very nice guy. Really.

NORMAND ROGER,[30] COMPOSER, *FATHER AND DAUGHTER*

We finished mixing *Father and Daughter* on a Friday night, and the deadline to submit it for the Ottawa Festival was the next day, Saturday, before noon, I think. There was not enough time to send the film by courier, and we decided to take the more or less two-hour drive from Montreal to Ottawa to deliver the film in person. *Father and Daughter* got selected and then received both audience and jury awards at the festival. That launched the film into an amazing series of prizes in most major animation festivals including the Oscar in the coming winter.

STEVE ROSE,[31] FILM CRITIC, *THE GUARDIAN*, *THE RED TURTLE* REVIEW

The story operates at the level of a universal myth, free of dialogue or specifics, subtly alluding to more essential, existential matters. The simple, uncluttered images do the rest. This is a movie to bask in, and we're given the space to do so. Characters are often dwarfed in lush expanses of sea, sky or forest, and there's a delight in small details: a Greek chorus of scuttling crabs, the lapping of waves on the shore. There are moments of violence, too – this is no therapeutic screensaver. The experience is captivating, transcendental even.

ISABEL STEVENS,[32] FILM CRITIC, BRITISH FILM INSTITUTE, *THE RED TURTLE* REVIEW

Pictures are the film's currency, and they are, without exaggeration, sublime. The film is a masterclass in chiaroscuro: shadows are just as intricately sketched as the life forms that cause them. Even from a distance, a bottle washed up on the beach has a lighter shadow than that of a human.

ISAO TAKAHATA,[33] DIRECTOR AND CO-FOUNDER, STUDIO GHIBLI, AND ARTISTIC PRODUCER, *THE RED TURTLE*

With *The Red Turtle*, Michael has succeeded again in depicting the truth of life, simply yet profoundly and with real heart. It is an astonishing accomplishment.

Humankind cannot live without maintaining a balanced relationship with nature founded upon equality and empathy. And in the eyes of this man, as is more or less clear to everyone, the red turtle is indeed his wife. This is how I understand Michael's message. I cannot express sufficiently my deep respect for, and identification with, the fact that there exists a powerful resonance, on the subject of man and nature, between the line that runs through all Michael's work and ideas that have existed in Japan since ancient times.

WILLEM THIJSSEN,[34] FILM PRODUCER, *FATHER AND DAUGHTER* AND *AROMA OF TEA*

Michael is the most adorable man I have ever met! He never lets you down, he is always inspiring, it is so easy to work with him, but he always says (in a kind way) his opinion! The moments I remember best are my visits to his house in London, and our talks about the construction of his own studio in the garden.

Such a great idea! Once he came to the city where I live, and he made a video of the passing bicycles as a part of research for *Father and Daughter*. The Dutch people ride bicycles in a different way than British people do!

PAUL WILLIAMS,[35] ANIMATOR, *THE RED TURTLE*

I feel that the magic of a film really comes together in post-production, when the music comes in, and the effects and compositing, and editing inches the film towards completion. The animation is only one part of the jigsaw, and I've often seen great animation not quite making the impact it should in a film, but for *The Red Turtle*, I feel that every part worked brilliantly together.

ARJAN WILSCHUT,[36] DIRECTOR AND ANIMATOR, CO-ANIMATOR, *FATHER AND DAUGHTER*

After our three months' collaboration on *Father and Daughter*, three thoughts had settled firmly in my head:

1. I've decided to move back to Holland. Working on the film made me realise how much I missed the Dutch landscape, my culture and my family.

2. I've decided to make my own short films. I never imagined I would make something as beautiful as *Father and Daughter*, but that wasn't the point. I just wanted to have a more personal relation to my work and my art.

3. I wanted to become a smarter and kinder person. Michael is not only a great artist; he is also an extremely friendly and intelligent person. His personality inspired me to change a few of my less charming character traits.

NOTES

1. Mikhail Aldashin's email to Andrijana Ružić, 16 October 2019.
2. Bendazzi, Giannalberto, *Animation: A World History*, Volume 3, Focal Press, New York, November 2015, p. 115.

3. Serge Besset's email to Andrijana Ružić, 19 January 2019.
4. Marco Bellano's email to Andrijana Ružić, 9 July 2019.
5. Bobrowska, Olga, *Emile Who? Before 1st European Animation Emile Awards Ceremony*, Zippy Frames, 7 December 2017, http://www.zippyframes.com/index.php/awards-prizes/emile-who-before-1st-european-animation-emil-awards-ceremony, retrieved on 5 October 2018.
6. Bruno Bozzetto's email to Andrijana Ružić, 27 October 2018.
7. Paola Bristot's email to Andrijana Ružić, 20 May 2018, from the unpublished paper presented at the international conference "Eulogy to Sublime – From Kant to Graphic Novel", Accademia di Belle Arti, Venice, 19–21 April 2018.
8. Rastko Ćirić's email to Andrijana Ružić, 5 October 2019.
9. Cotte, Olivier, *Secrets of Oscar-Winning Animation*, Focal Press, New York and London, 2006, p. 245.
10. Debruge, Peter, *Film Review: The Red Turtle*, 18 May 2016, https://variety.com/2016/film/reviews/the-red-turtle-review-studio-ghibli-la-tortue-rouge-1201777707/, retrieved 11 April 2019.
11. Guy Delisle's email to Andrijana Ružić, 7 August 2017.
12. Bordo's email to Andrijana Ružić, 23 September 2017.
13. Paul Driessen's email to Andrijana Ružić, 14 July 2018.
14. Piotr Dumała's email to Andrijana Ružić, 21 September 2019.
15. *Interview with Pascale Ferran*, Press Kit, Wild Bunch International Sales, https://www.wildbunch.biz/movie/the-red-turtle/, retrieved 2 February 2018.
16. Igor Grubić's email to Andrijana Ružić, 18 November 2019.
17. Heath, Paul, *The Red Turtle review*, 18 May 2016, http://www.thehollywoodnews.com/2016/05/18/the-red-turtle-review-cannes/, retrieved 11 April 2019
18. Claire Jennings's email to Andrijana Ružić, 1 May 2019.
19. Céline Kélépikis's email to Andrijana Ružić, 27 March 2018.
20. BBC Radio 5 Live, https://www.youtube.com/watch?v=uOJMPcxhdok, retrieved 20 December 2018.
21. Igor Kovalyov's email to Andrijana Ružić, 12 November 2018.
22. *Interview with Jean-Christophe Lie*, Press Kit, Wild Bunch International Sales, https://www.wildbunch.biz/movie/the-red-turtle/, retrieved 2 February 2018.
23. Julien De Man's email to Andrijana Ružić, 8 April 2018.
24. Simone Massi's email to Andrijana Ružić, 4 September 2019.
25. Laurent Perez del Mar's email to Andrijana Ružić, 27 July 2017.

26. *Prima Linea' s report*, Press Kit, Wild Bunch International Sales, https://www.wildbunch.biz/movie/the-red-turtle/, retrieved 2 February 2018.
27. Jill Purdum's email to Andrijana Ružić, 22 March 2019.
28. Purves, Barry J. C., *Stop Motion: Passion, Process and Performance*, Focal Press, New York and London, 2007, p. 288.
29. Robinson, Chris, *The Animation Pimp*, AWN Press, Los Angeles, 2007, p. 340.
30. Normand Roger's email to Andrijana Ružić, 9 August 2017.
31. Rose, Steve, *The Red Turtle review: A Desert Island Movie to Bask*, *The Guardian*, 25 May 2017, https://www.theguardian.com/film/2017/may/25/the-red-turtle-review-a-desert-island-movie-to-bask-in, retrieved 11 April 2019.
32. Stevens, Isabel, *The Red Turtle: First Look*, BFI, 23 September 2016, https://www.bfi.org.uk/news-opinion/sight-sound-magazine/reviews-recommendations/red-turtle-first-look, retrieved 11 April 2019.
33. *Interview with Isao Takahata*, Press Kit, Wild Bunch International Sales, https://www.wildbunch.biz/movie/the-red-turtle/, retrieved 2 February 2018.
34. Willem Thijssen's email to Andrijana Ružić, 13 September 2017.
35. Paul Williams's email to Andrijana Ružić, 24 September 2019.
36. Arjan Wilschut's email to Andrijana Ružić, 28 September 2017.

Appendix 5

Filmography

The Interview (1978)
graduation film
Duration: 8 minutes

Tom Sweep (1992)
pilot film

Design, story and direction:	Michael Dudok de Wit
Animation:	Michael Dudok de Wit, Anne Justice, Craig Baxter
Music:	Graham Henderson, Neil Arthur
Production:	Jill Thomas/Richard Purdum Productions
Duration:	2 min 30

The Monk and the Fish (1994)

Story, design, backgrounds:	Michael Dudok de Wit
Animation:	Michael Dudok de Wit, Guy Delisle
Director:	Michael Dudok de Wit
Music:	Serge Besset's arrangement of the La Folìa by Corelli
Editor:	Hervé Guichard
Mix:	Jean-Claude Millet
Production studio:	Folimage
Producers:	Jacques-Rémy Girerd, Patrick Eveno
Duration:	6 min 30

Father and Daughter (2000)

Story, design, backgrounds:	Michael Dudok de Wit
Animation:	Michael Dudok de Wit, Arjan Wilschut
Director:	Michael Dudok de Wit
Music:	Normand Roger with the collaboration of Denis Chartrand
Mix:	Studio SPR, Montreal
Sound:	Jean-Baptiste Roger
Production studio:	CinéTé Filmproductie Bv/ Cloudrunner LtD.
Producers:	Willem Thijssen, Claire Jennings
Duration:	8 min 30

The Aroma of Tea (2006)

Written, painted (with tea) and directed:	Michael Dudok de Wit
Technical direction, compositing:	Marc Schopman
Sound editing:	Nic Gill
Music:	Archangelo Corelli, Concerti grossi Op. 6, Nos. 2 and 12
Production:	Willem Thijssen/CinéTé Filmproductie Bv
Duration:	3 min 30

The Red Turtle (2016)

Director:	Michael Dudok de Wit
Screenplay:	Michael Dudok de Wit
Adaptation:	Pascale Ferran and Michael Dudok de Wit
Design:	Michael Dudok de Wit
Music:	Laurent Perez del Mar
Artistic producer:	Isao Takahata
Animation studio:	Prima Linea Productions
Producers:	Toshio Suzuki, Vincent Maraval, Pascal Caucheteux, Grégoire Sorlat, Béatrice Mauduit, co-producer: Leon Perahia
Line producers:	Valérie Schermann and Christophe Jankovic
First assistant director:	Jean-Pierre Bouchet
Storyboard:	Michael Dudok de Wit
Animation supervisor:	Jean-Christophe Lie
Clean up supervisor:	Marie Bouchet
Layout supervisor:	Eric Briche
Background supervisor:	Julien De Man
Colour supervisor:	Emma McCann
Shadow animator:	Pascal Herbreteau
Compositing supervisors:	Jean-Pierre Bouchet, Arnaud Bois
Special effects supervisor:	Mouloud Oussid
Editor:	Céline Kélépikis
Digital colour grading:	Peter Bernaers
Sound supervisor:	Bruno Seznec
Sound mixer:	Fabien Devillers
Sound editor:	Matthieu Michaux
Sound design:	Alexandre Fleurant, Sébastien Marquilly
Foley artist:	Florian Fabre
Sound:	Piste Rouge
Duration:	80 min

a Why Not Productions – Wild Bunch – Studio Ghibli – CN4 Productions – Arte France Cinema – Belvision Coproduction – with the support of Eurimages – with the participation of Canal+ – Ciné+ – Arte France – Region Poitou-Charentes – Departement de la Charente – Region Wallonne – Fondation Gan pour le cinema – in association with Cinemage 9 – Palatine Etoile 11 – Palatine Etoile 12 – BNP Paribas Fortis Film Finance

SELECTION OF COMMERCIALS (1980–2001)

- Actifed Germ (Richard Purdum Productions) for Wellcome Foundation
- Heinz Egg (Richard Purdum Productions) for Heinz
- The Long Sleep (Richard Purdum Productions) for Macallan Whiskey
- VW Sunrise (Richard Purdum Productions) for Volkswagen
- Smart Illusions (Richard Purdum Productions) for Nestlé
- Pink Foot (Richard Purdum Productions) for Owens Corning
- *AT&T* (Acme Filmworks) 6 commercials for AT&T
- A Life (Acme Filmworks) for United

FREELANCING FOR OTHER FILMMAKERS

- *Heavy Metal* (1981) feature film directed by Gerald Potterton (animator)
- *Beauty and the Beast* (1989) storyboard reel of the early version produced by Richard Purdum Productions (Storyboarder) later produced (1992) by Walt Disney Studios and directed by Kirk Wise and Gary Trousdale
- *Mickey's Audition* (1992) short film directed by Rob Minkoff (animator)
- *Prince Cinders* (1993) short film directed by Derek W. Hayes (animator)
- *T.R.A.N.S.I.T* (1998) short film directed by Piet Kroon (animator)
- *L'Enfant au Grelot* (1998) feature film by Jacques-Rémy Girerd (animator)
- *Fantasia 2000* (1999) feature film directed by Eric Goldberg, James Algar, Don Hahn, Gaëtan Brizzi, Hendel Butoy, Pixote Hunt, Francis Glebas, Paul Brizzi (animator)

- *The Canterbury Tales/The Knight's Tale* (1999) short film directed by Dave Antrobus and Mic Graves (animator)
- *La Prophétie des Grenouilles* (2003) feature film by Jacques-Rémy Girerd (animator)

Bibliography

BOOKS

Bendazzi, Giannalberto, *Animation: A World History*, Focal Press, New York, 2015.

Bendazzi, Giannalberto, *Animazione, Una storia universale*, UTET, Milano, 2017.

Bendazzi, Giannalberto, *Lezioni sul cinema d'animazione*, CUEM, Milano, 2004.

Bendazzi, G., Cecconello, M., Michelone, G., *Coloriture. Voci, rumori, musiche nel cinema d'animazione*, Pendragon, Bologna, 1995.

Cotte, Olivier, *Secrets of Oscar-Winning Animation*, Focal Press, New York and London, 2006.

Dudok de Wit, Michael, *Vader en Dochter*, Leopold, Amsterdam, 2015.

Faber, Liz, Walters, Helen, *Animation Unlimited: Innovative Short Films Since 1940*, Laurence King Publishing Ltd, London, 2004.

Focillon, Henri, *Piero della Francesca*, Abscondita, Milano, 2004.

Furniss, Maureen, *The Animation Bible*, Abrams, New York, 2008.

Furniss, Maureen, *Art in Motion: Animation Aesthetics*, Revised Edition, John Libbey Publishing, Eastleigh, 2007.

Ghez, Didier, *Walt's People*, Volume 9, Interview with Tom Sito, Xlibris Corporation, Bloomington, 2010.

Gombrich, Ernst H., *Art and Illusion. A Study in the Psychology of Pictorial Representation*, Pantheon Books, New York, 1960.

Gorbman, Claudia, *Unheard Melodies: Narrative Film Music*, BFI Publishing, London and Indiana University Press, Bloomington, 1987.

Hemingway, Ernest, *Death in the Afternoon*, Scribner Classics, New York, 1999.

Kawa-Topor, Xavier, Nguyên, Ilan, *Michael Dudok de Wit. Le cinéma d'animation sensible. Entretien avec le réalisateur de La Tortue Rouge*, Capricci, Paris, 2019.

Kitson, Clare, *British Animation: The Channel 4 Factor*, Parliament Hill Publishing, London, 2008.

Kitson, Clare, *Yuri Norstein and Tale of Tales. An Animator's Journey*, Indiana University Press, Bloomington, 2005.

Kurosawa, Akira, *Something Like an Autobiography*, Vintage Books, New York, 1983.

Lazić, Radoslav, *Režija filmske animacije*, Autorska izdanja, Beograd, 2012.

Lenburg, Jeff, *Who's Who in Animated Cartoons: An International Guide to Film and Television's Award-Winning and Legendary Animators*, Applause Books, New York, 2006.

Merlin, Geneviève, *Michael Dudok de Wit. La Tortue Rouge*, Atlande, Neuilly, 2018.

Miyazaki, Hayao, *Starting Point: 1979–1996*, Viz Media, San Francisco, 2009.

Munari, Bruno, *Arte come mestiere*, Gius. Laterza & Figli, Bari, 2018.

Munitić, Ranko, *Estetika animacije*, Vedis, Zagreb, 2012.

Pilling, Jayne, *2D and Beyond*, RotoVision SA, Mies, 2001.

Perroni, Sergio Claudio, *Entro a volte nel tuo sonno*, La Nave di Teseo, 2018.

Purves, Barry J. C., *Stop Motion: Passion, Process and Performance*, Focal Press, New York and London, 2007.

Richie, Donald, *The Films of Akira Kurosawa*, University of California Press, Berkeley and Los Angeles, 1996.

Robinson, Chris, *The Animation Pimp*, AWN Press, Los Angeles, 2007.

Sudović, Zlatko, Munitić, Ranko, *Zagrebački krug crtanog filma*, Volume 4, Zavod za kulturu Hrvatske, Zagreb, 1986.

Taniguchi, Jiro, *La montagna magica*, Rizzoli-Lizard, Milano, 2009.

Walser, Robert, *Oppressive Light*. Selected poems translated and edited by Daniele Pantano, Black Lawrence Press, Schaeferstunde/Tryst, 2012.

Wells, Paul, *Animation. Genre and Authorship*, Wallflower Press, London, 2002.

Wells, Paul, Quin, Joanna, Mills, Les, *Basics Animation 03: Drawing for Animation*, An AVA Book, Lausanne, 2009.

INTERNET RESOURCES: ARTICLES

Alzial, Sylvain, *Une musique pour Loulou*, interview with Laurent Perez del Mar, 13 December 2017, http://www.maisondelaradio.fr/article/une-musique-pour-loulou, retrieved 15 January 2018.

Bacher, Hans, *Beauty and the Beast 1989, Animation Treasures*, 2 October 2009, https://one1more2time3.wordpress.com/2009/02/10/london-1989/, retrieved 17 December 2018.

Barlow, Dominic, *The Red Turtle*, interview with Michael Dudok de Wit, 4:3, 20 September 2016, https://fourthreefilm.com/2016/09/the-red-turtle-an-interview-with-michael-dudok-de-wit/, retrieved 4 September 2018.

Baseel, Casey, *Hayao Miyazaki slams anime, hints at comeback, and praises The Red Turtle, all in one breath*, SoraNews24, 2 September 2016, https://en.rocketnews24.com/2016/09/02/hayao-miyazaki-slams-anime-hints-at-comeback-and-praises-the-red-turtle-and-all-in-one-breath/, retrieved 10 February 2018.

Blondeau, Thomas, *Laurent Perez del Mar*, Ecran Total No. 1099, 29 June 2016, https://www.laurentperezdelmar.com/documents/Ecran-Total-DEF.JPG

Desowitz, Bill, *The Red Turtle: How the Animator Oscar Contender Handled Conflict*, IndieWire, 21 February 2017, http://www.indiewire.com/2017/02/the-red-turtle-oscar-video-1201785366/.

Digital Arts Staff, *Michael Dudok de Wit on Directing Studio Ghibli's New Film "The Red Turtle"*, 13 June 2017, https://www.digitalartsonline.co.uk/features/motion-graphics/interview-michael-dudok-de-wit-on-directing-studio-ghiblis-new-film-red-turtle/, retrieved 10 September 2017.

Dreyfus, Stéphane, *Takahata – Dudok de Wit: Rencontre au sommet*, 25 November 2016, https://film-animation.blogs.la-croix.com/takahata-dudok-de-wit-rencontre-au-sommet/2016/11/25/, retrieved 6 May 2019.

Dudok de Wit, Alex, *Notes from a Small Island*, Sight and Sound, June 2017, http://www.primalinea.com/latortuerouge/revuepresse/Sight_Sound-1706.pdf, retrieved 10 March 2018.

Fear, David, *Rolling Stone*, 23 January 2017, http://www.rollingstone.com/movies/reviews/the-red-turtle-movie-review-w461064, retrieved on 5 November 2017.

Genin, Bernard, *Interview with Michael Dudok de Wit*, Press Kit Wild Bunch. International Sales, https://www.wildbunch.biz/movie/the-red-turtle/, retrieved 2 February 2018.

Halfyard, Kurt, *Interview: The Red Turtle Director Michael Dudok de Wit Talks Studio Ghibli and More*, Screenanarchy, 26 January 2017, http://screenanarchy.com/2017/01/interview-the-red-turtle-director-michael-dudok-de-wit-talks-studio-ghibli-and-more.html, retrieved 10 April 2018.

Hofferman, Jon, *Laurent Perez del Mar receives IFMCA award for The Red Turtle*, http://filmmusiccritics.org/2017/03/laurent-perez-del-mar-receives-ifmca-award-for-the-red-turtle/, retrieved 2 November 2017.

Hofferman, Jon, *Sound of Animation: An Interview with Normand Roger*, World Network, 2008, https://www.awn.com/animationworld/sound-animation-interview-normand-roger, retrieved 25 July 2018.

Hourigan, Jonathan, *A Conversation with Michael Dudok de Wit*, http://www.robert-bresson.com/Words/Dudok_de_Wit.html, retrieved 9 October 2019.

Koller, M. John, *Ox Herding: Stages of Zen Practice*, http://www.columbia.edu/cu/weai/exeas/resources/pdf/oxherding.pdf, retrieved on 11 May 2019.

Lerner, Ben, *A Strange Australian Masterpiece*, The New Yorker, 29 March 2017, https://www.newyorker.com/books/page-turner/a-strange-australian-masterpiece/, retrieved 5 January 2020.

Loughrey, Clarisse, *The Red Turtle: Director Michael Dudok de Wit on his unique collaboration with the Studio Ghibli*, Independent, 30 May 2017, http://www.independent.co.uk/arts-entertainment/films/features/the-red-turtle-studio-ghibli-michael-dudok-de-wit-interview-animation-cannes-2016-release-date-a7763506.html, retrieved 10 February 2018.

McAllister, James, *Songs of the Sea. Exploring the Soundscape of The Red Turtle*, The London Economic, 25 September 2017, https://www.thelondoneconomic.com/film/songs-sea-exploring-soundscape-red-turtle/25/09/, retrieved 27 September 2017.

Mitchell, Ben, *The Films of Michael Dudok de Wit–Interview and Competiton*, Skwigly Online Animation Magazine, 31 July 2018, http://www.skwigly.co.uk/michael-dudok-de-wit/, retrieved 21 September 2018.

Molinhoff, Sara, *A Beautiful Language*, The Oxonian Review, 11 May 2009, http://www.oxonianreview.org/wp/a-beautiful-language/, retrieved 7 May 2019.

Sarto, Dan, *Michael Dudok de Wit Talks "The Red Turtle" and Partnership with Studio Ghibli*, 10 February 2017, https://www.awn.com/animationworld/micha-l-dudok-de-wit-talks-red-turtle-and-partnership-studio-ghibli, retrieved 30 September 2017.

Schweiger, Daniel, *Interview with Laurent Perez del Mar*, Film Music Magazine, 20 March 2018, http://www.filmmusicmag.com/?p=18620, retrieved 21 March 2018.

Shimoda, Todd, *"Oh" a Mystery of "mono no aware"*, https://ohthenovel.wordpress.com/mononoaware/, retrieved 21 October 2018.

Smurthwaite, Nick, *One Man and his Wobbly Dog*, The Guardian, 20 April 2001, https://www.theguardian.com/film/2001/apr/20/culture.features2, retrieved 13 December 2018.

Sporn, Michael, *Animated Oscars*, 13 November 2006, http://www.michaelspornanimation.com/splog/?p=847, retrieved 3 November 2018.

Thomas, Lou, *The Red Turtle: The Films That Influenced Studio Ghibli's Latest Spellbinder*, BFI, 26 May 2017, http://www.bfi.org.uk/news-opinion/news-bfi/red-turtle-studio-ghibli-michael-dudok-wit-influences, retrieved 10 April 2018.

Valentino, Andrea, *Could La Folia be history's most enduring tune?* BBC Culture, 31 July 2019, http://www.bbc.com/culture/story/20190726-could-la-folia-be-historys-most-enduring-tune, retrieved 6 September 2019.

Wild Bunch International Sales, *Interview with Jean-Christophe Lie*, Press Kit, https://www.wildbunch.biz/movie/the-red-turtle/, retrieved 29 January 2018.

Wild Bunch International Sales, *Interview with Isao Takahata*, Press Kit, https://www.wildbunch.biz/movie/the-red-turtle/, retrieved 10 February 2018.

Zhuo-Ning Su, *The Red Turtle director talks working with Studio Ghibli*, Storytelling Sans Dialogue and More, 17 October 2016, https://thefilmstage.com/features/the-red-turtle-director-talks-working-with-studio-ghibli-animating-sans-dialogue-more/, retrieved 3 December 2017.

VIDEO (VIMEO, YOU TUBE):

Contender Conversations, *The Red Turtle—Michael Dudok de Wit "Intuition vs Reason"*, https://www.youtube.com/watch?v=Ir45I0pCu6M, retrieved 7 December 2017.

Courant, Gérard, *Michael Dudok de Wit* (1997), Cinématon #1865, https://www.youtube.com/watch?v=rivTJnRQgmg, retrieved 7 December 2017.

Michael Dudok de Wit in Teachers TV: Reading a film *The Monk and the Fish*, https://www.youtube.com/watch?v=s9dHJro69f4, retrieved 26 February 2019.

TV Interview with Michael Dudok de Wit. ARTE, Court-circuit, https://www.youtube.com/watch?v=R9abaZwPNLA&t=456s, June of 2006, retrieved 9 December 2017. *United: Michael Dudok de Wit*, https://vimeo.com/29664893, retrieved 1 March 2018.

Whitney, Mark, Carl Gustav Jung in documentary film *Matter of Heart* (1983) https://www.youtube.com/watch?v=lxXyTrdgJKg&index=1&list=FLHaRozXuHcnLE8UCP4mQXPg&t=1984s, retrieved in 15 February 2018.

DVD:

Arakawa, Kaku, documentary film *Never-Ending Man—Hayao Miyazaki*, NHK, 2017.

Doebele, Thomas, Schmidt, Maarten, documentary film *Het Verlangen van Michael Dudok de Wit*, VPRO, 2016.

Index